NUDGES *from the* OTHER SIDE

TRUE STORIES OF AFTER-LIFE COMMUNICATION

RECEIVE HEART-CENTERED HOPE AND COMFORT.
YOU *CAN* CONNECT WITH YOUR LOVED ONES AFTER
THEY'VE CROSSED OVER.

MARY CONNAUGHTY-SULLIVAN

Mary Connaughty-Sullivan

→ Love ↘
Peace 🌸 Comfort
↳ Hope ↙

Red Penguin BOOKS

What Readers Are Saying

"In sharing her own and others' experiences of 'nudges from the other side,' Connaughty-Sullivan invites you to join her as a co-traveler. Whether you are just beginning your grief journey, are a seasoned navigator trudging forward, or find yourself retracing steps on a path eerily similar but uniquely different from one you've walked before, she is a credible guide. This book has found its way to you for a reason, whether you know it or not; Mary's story has a message meant for you. If you read with your mind and your heart open, embracing the familiar and the foreign with equal vigor, you may encounter in these pages possibilities you want to be real, truths you know to be so, and hope that sustains them both."

~Margaret T. Gilbride, JD, CT, Assistant Professor and Director of Grief and Loss Projects at The Boggs Center, Rutgers University

"*Especially to a parent, Mary's story first catapults us into groundless chasms of shock and horror; and then, as we catch our breath, the thought 'Thank God this didn't happen to me and mine' offers some bit of relief. But we know that her story must become ours, one way or another, as every object we hold dear eventually will be taken from us as we die. What is never lost is what we really are, or more accurately, what is us— source, awareness, consciousness, spirit, God or whatever you choose to call it. As Mary proclaims, this book is about hope. She offers a mother's assurance that there is a path through unimaginable loss, and by opening to the vastness and mystery of that which we truly are, that pathway illuminates ourselves and the entire world. May those in need of this message find this book.*"

~George J. Felos, J.D. – George is a national expert in end-of-life cases, was a Hospice patient volunteer and Board Chair of the world's largest non-profit Hospice, and presents *Meditation for Lawyers®*, an accredited continuing-education course teaching attorneys how to meditate.

"*Mary's book is a lovingly compiled testament to the connection that lives on far beyond the limits of an earthly death. It is filled with meaningful quotes and references but most importantly, the signs and messages she clearly and directly received after the passing of her son. The book will be helpful to others whether they are dealing with a loved one's death, or simply interested in what lies beyond the veil.*"

~Stormy May, Compassionate Communication With Horses

"*Mary writes in the unapologetically raw way that will be immediately recognizable and resonant to anyone experiencing profound loss. By sharing unedited passages directly from a decade of highly personal journals, she courageously invites the reader into the devastation she faced with the loss of her son, and the unorthodox path she took to find healing and even a new version of happiness. Read. Weep. Smile. And heal your own losses. Mary shows us how.*"

~Molly Sargent, Founder/CEO, ProImpress

"A magnificent and magical true story. Mary and Aaron's is a rare and moving journey of love, loss, faith, wonder and transformation. Mix in an intriguing thread of divine coincidences—which Einstein called 'God's way of remaining anonymous'—and you have an unforgettable story that lifts you from the depths of despair around the loss of a loved one to the highest heights of hope, belief and transcendence. Every time you see a dragonfly from now on, you'll be reminded of the eternal love woven through every glimmer of life."

~Matthew K. Cross, CEO, LeadershipAlliance.com

"Nudges from the Other Side is a guidebook for navigating the unspeakable journey of surviving the death of a child. Mary gently brings the reader through her own experience, sharing the utter individuality and specificity of each family, each child. She allows and invites the reader into her life, providing opportunity for other bereaved parents and people to find themselves in her experiences with Aaron, during his terrestrial life, as well as the ongoing relationship that she has with him still. I will be providing this book as a Book Club offering to one of the Bereaved Parents groups that I work with, and I know that it will provide immense connection and validation to those of us who also continue nurturing deep connections with our children as they navigate the 'after' life. Mary's courage and commitment to follow the path that was her truth, inspires strength and persistence. Her authenticity and vulnerability are poetically shared, and this book will be seen as a 'How To' guide for paying attention, being aware of the signs, and refusing to talk ourselves out of them. I highly recommend this book for the bereaved, and also those who love them."

~Stacy Morataya-Pilkington, Executive Recruiter & Moderator, *Bereaved Parents of Childhood Cancer*

"A well-crafted book with a lot of scope to touch the minds and hearts of readers across all ages! The subtle interweaving of emotion with reality and its dark side adds that extra touch of inspiration! Good luck to the author for the success of the book."

~Katherine Abraham, author of *Every Sunset Has A Story*

Acknowledgments

Grateful acknowledgement is made to the following:

New World Library, Novato, CA (www.newworldlibrary.com) for permission to reprint excerpts from *Horses and the Mystical Path* by Adele von Rüst McCormick, Marlena Deborah McCormick, and Thomas E. McCormick. Copyright © 2004.

Rosemary Altea for permission to reprint excerpts from *The Eagle and the Rose: A Remarkable True Story*. Copyright © 1995.

Jennifer Louden for permission to reprint an article from her newsletter on the "Shero's Journey."

Christine Sang, Interspecies Communicator, for permission to include her conversation with Aaron after he passed. Christine can be found at AnimalAwakening.com.

For Aaron, of course.

Contents

Author's Note

The premise of this book lies in the Laws of Thermodynamics. Specifically, the first law which essentially states that matter (energy being a property of matter) can neither be created nor destroyed. I realize it sounds strange to hear that a book that chronicles a mother's grief journey ends up resting on a law of physics, but it does. You see, along this unwanted journey I discovered that although my son was no longer physically in my presence, he was still alive and well, and he was letting me know it over and over again.

I discovered that there's so much more to life and death than we learn during our time in school and from our parents and other influencers, and I found that others like me also had their own stories to tell. In that, I realized the greatest gift I could share with the world is Hope. And that's the purpose of sharing my journey with you.

Prologue

May 31, 2010 - Memorial Day

I woke that morning to hear a soft rain pattering on the roof of our horse trailer. It seemed our long weekend of horse camping would end early. We wouldn't set out on a ride in the rain. It was always OK if it started raining once we were on the trail, but our mantra was to never deliberately start out in the rain. We'd had a lovely weekend filled with fun rides and good times with our friends, so no matter. I glanced over at Dan still sleeping peacefully and decided I'd go clean the stalls and let him have some rest.

When I returned from the barn about 45 minutes later, it was raining harder, and as I stepped into our living quarters, Dan was frantic. He reported that it looked as if he'd had at least 20 calls on his phone and that something must be dreadfully wrong at home. He needed to run up to higher ground to try to get a signal. As he slung on his rain slicker, he told me to hurry and get the trailer buttoned up so we could leave quickly. I did as he asked, and as I worked, I imagined that our house had burned down. I specifically remember thinking of our kids, and assuring myself they were ok and specifically that my son, Aaron, was self-sufficient and was certainly alright. Yes, it surely had to be a big problem with the house, but never mind, I knew we could sort those types of things out.

Suddenly, the door flung open and Dan's face was filled with shock. I remember demanding he tell me what was going on, but he simply couldn't speak. He just shook his head and sank as his legs began to buckle. I have no idea what possessed me to ask this question as I put my hands on his arms, but looking him straight in the eyes, I asked, "Is it Aaron?" He could only shake his head yes. My instant question came out as a whispered hiss, "Is he dead?" Dan nodded his head wordlessly. "Yesssss..."

SILENCE.

There were a few seconds of deafening silence, almost as if all time had simply stopped, and we were in a bubble of nothingness. Utterly devoid of sound, life, and reality. Our eyes were locked and the only thing I can remember saying is, "You can NOT fall apart on me now." I was too stunned to cry, wail, or even fall over. I went into some sort of automaton mode: all I knew was that I needed him to get us home. I willed Dan—my hero—to come about. And he did.

It was a hard load with the horses in the driving rain, and we exchanged very few words as we drove home in stunned silence, each of us wordlessly contemplating a reality without my son in it. A couple hours later, we pulled into our driveway. We left the horses standing on the trailer as people began streaming from the house to meet us. These exchanges still sound like hollow shrieks in my head:

Dan's ex-wife: "An accident on the road in the early morning hours. We came as soon as we got word... No, he didn't hit anyone else... No, Sam wasn't with him."

Matthew, Dan's son, my dear stepson: "It's my fault, Mary. I'm so sorry. IT'S *MY* FAULT."

The police officer: "He didn't look bad, but you shouldn't

go to the morgue to see him… There will be an investigation; we'll be in touch soon."

Peter, Dan's son and Aaron's best friend and co-conspirator in everything fun: "We don't know where he was going… We don't know why he left the house."

Me screaming to random kids sitting in my living room: "Get out of my house, all of you."

Dan: "Mary, go lie down."

DARKNESS.

HELPLESSNESS.

And finally, **RESOLVE**.

"I'm going to see him," I announced at the foot of the stairs a few hours after I'd been sent to bed. "I'll understand if no one wants to come with me. I'll welcome anyone who does."

Dan, whom I believe wouldn't leave my side if I jumped into a lake of fire, said he'd drive. Megan, Dan's daughter, got up and came along. I think she'd jump right into that lake of fire to save me too.

We were ushered into a private room (that I now know was not the morgue) where Aaron lay on a metal stretcher draped from the shoulders down in a thickly starched sheet. His shoulders were smooth and toned, and I didn't see a scratch on him. His eyes were almost shut, but I could still see the expression in them and on his face. Not of shock, horror, or impending doom, but rather one of anticipation. I later realized it was the same look he had on his face every time we were pulling him up out of the water on his wakeboard on a shimmering summer day. Anticipation of a good ride. As much as I could appreciate anything that awful day, I liked that. I kissed his sweet face, Dan did too, and I remember Megan running her fingers gently along the top of his head. I've never regretted going to the hospital that day.

I've always been glad and grateful that Dan and Megan came too.

I wasn't OK. But I was resolved. Resolved to somehow get this right. This experience I never wanted to have—I somehow needed to honor him by getting it right. And getting it right meant doing it my way and on my terms. I don't know how or why I knew that, but I didn't deny any of my early thoughts or revelations. In fact, I resolved to experience it honestly and truthfully.

Later on, I finally could cry. My beautiful, funny, smart boy was gone from my time. My unwanted grief journey was underway.

I have refused to live
locked in the orderly house of
reasons and proofs.
The world I live in and believe in
is wider than that. And anyway,
What's wrong with Maybe?
You wouldn't believe what once or
twice I have seen. I'll just
tell you this:
only if there are angels in your head will you
ever, possibly, see one.
~Mary Oliver (*The World I Live In*)

In my own words, penned a couple years after Aaron's death, I wrote this in the rapidly filling journal I was keeping:

"This journal is filled with instances where I felt Aaron was nudging us from heaven—to let us know he was alive and well. I jotted them down

because I never wanted to later on second guess that they really never happened just the way that I wrote them down."

Someone I loved once gave me a box full of darkness.
It took me years to understand that this too, was a gift.
~Mary Oliver ("The Uses of Sorrow," *Thirst*)

Firsts

Take one day at a time; one moment at a time. Sometimes just one breath at a time.

This was advice given to me by a complete stranger that in the weeks following Aaron's passing (I hate using the word *death*) that I leaned on and lived by. It made sense to me to not try to think further ahead than the next place I'd set down my foot or inhale my next breath. I didn't have anything else in me that could even operate beyond those steps and those individual breaths.

I allowed that to be OK.

At the same time, I marveled that the sun still came up every morning. The sky was blue, sometimes it rained; and everyone else was going about their business. But my world had just collapsed. Yet I could see no one else felt that crushing, overbearing, awful despair that infiltrated my very soul. For some reason, I marveled at that too.

Micro-awareness, and all-consuming grief: my new, unwavering, unwanted companions in those dark first days.

Isn't that what hope is?
Not a wish, not a specific thing that you pray will be delivered to you, but merely an expectation that whatever dark, sleety side of the road you might find yourself on will not last forever.
~Elizabeth Letts (*The Ride of Her Life: The True Story of a Woman, Her Horse, and Their Last Chance Journey Across America*)

Survival

I had a lot of random thoughts early on. I interacted with very few people, but some of them gave me words I could cling to. Some thoughts came from what I read or heard, and some came from that reservoir none of us are really aware of deep inside of our own beings.

Life sometimes gives you second chances.
When you decide something with an open heart, you usually make the right decision.
Even amongst the hurts of life, love prevails.
~Maya Angelou

This verse gave me some solace: "Let the morning bring me word of your unfailing love, for I have put my trust in you. Show me the way I should go, for to you I lift up my soul." *Psalm 143:8.*

Sam, Aaron's dog, said through an animal communicator: "Maternal love is like a soft breeze over the heart." The communicator indicated that Sam felt it from me towards her and it was also very connected to Aaron.

I was hunting for tiny blotches of sunshine to bring a small measure of warmth to a heart that felt like it had all but stopped beating. This could be the most raw and innate definition of optimism. At the very least, it was survival.

So, I allowed those words, "Take one day at a time; one moment at a time; sometimes just one breath at a time," to give me comfort. They were the tiniest filament of a lifeline, but a lifeline, nonetheless. They made me realize that even when our world closes in on us, there is still something tethering us to love, hope, truth, courage, and strength.

Journaling

I took to journaling my thoughts early on. Friends and family insisted I go to grief counseling, go to church, see a psychologist, read certain books, and perform certain behaviors to rid myself of the sadness and prevent me from sinking into an unrecoverable depression. None of the ideas sounded like anything I wanted to do. I spotted an empty journal someone had once given me as a gift. I'd never made so much as a scratch in it. But I picked it up and began pouring my thoughts, feelings, and experiences into it. Sometimes I wrote about how I was feeling that day, sometimes I wrote about experiences that seemed impossibly surreal, yet they happened just exactly as I recorded them in the journal. Thirteen years hence, I'm still writing in the second volume of my journal. Not quite as often as in those early days, but when something happens or when a thought strikes me as important.

Many of the experiences that I had, especially in those first few years, defy logic, science, and common sensibility. I was grateful for what happened because I believed it was a nudge from the other side—Aaron letting me know he was alive and well and that he wanted me to know it and feel at peace. As the years wore on, I began collecting other people's stories that were equally as uncommon, surprising, and heart-warming. No one whom I've asked if I could include their story in my book has ever turned me down.

I'm really glad that I took the path I did because not only did the journaling give me an outlet and a measure of comfort in the moment, but it chronicled instances I may have forgotten, or even worse, things I may have second-guessed as fantasies I created. But in fact, all of this is real—it happened just as I recorded it—and my desire is that it brings peace, hope, and comfort to those who need it most.

As you read through the following pages, note that italicized entries are taken word for word from my journals. You'll note that I often wrote directly to Aaron, and at times in the third person. Aaron was constantly on my mind, and I still keep a dialogue with him today, albeit not so frequently as in those first dark days and years.

The quotes I share herein are things I've come across that were extremely comforting and helpful to me. Many of them completely gripped my heart with the synchronicity they paralleled to my own thoughts and experience. I've indicated instances where I have not been able to determine who the author is. All other unitalicized entries are my narration and are intended to provide additional detail to augment the journal entries.

The Lord is near to the brokenhearted and saves those who
are crushed in spirit.
~Psalm 34:18

Journal One

6/29/2010

> Aaron would not want me to be
> sad all the time.
> Think about WWAD bracelet!
>
> Give thanks for the things that are
> good that day. There are at
> last small blessings every day.

*The "WWAD bracelet" I refer to was a yellow and gray
rubber bracelet that one of Aaron's friends had made for the
funeral. It resonated with me to think about it not in terms of
what Aaron would do, but what would Aaron want me to do. I
felt certain he would not want me to be overwhelmed with
grief.

*The grief that I feel sits on my chest like a heavy blanket. At times I feel
as if I can't get enough breath in my lungs.*

*All around me, life goes on. Meanwhile, I can barely breathe. I can't
think about the future, next month, next week, or even the next hour.*

*I miss you so badly, and I think about all the things I could've done better
and another thorn pierces my heart.*

*Then I wonder if I'm hurting you now with my despair and I want to try
to honor you by doing this the right way, but I don't know how to not feel
like I do.*

That journal entry was so raw that even as I read it today, I'm
taken back to the overwhelming despair, hopelessness, and
helplessness I felt over a situation that was completely outside
of my control to change or even to influence in some tiny way.
It took me quite a while to stop looking for ways to get Aaron
back and to come to the realization that in fact the only thing
I had even one ounce of control over was my own attitude.

As I mentioned earlier, I wrote a lot of journal entries **to**
Aaron in those days. It made me feel connected to him to be
talking conversationally versus merely writing down the
thoughts that were swirling in my head. It sort of made me
feel like I was carrying on a chat with him via text (which was
a rather new method of communication back in 2010). As
you'll see in the following pages, he often nudged me back.
Not via text, but in many unusual ways—always ways that I'm
glad I wrote down because I know I now wouldn't believe they
really happened just as I recorded them, and the practical,
pragmatic me would discount them as imaginations of a torn
and tortured mind.

7/10/2010

My dearest Aaron:

It seems you are always a part of a running dialogue that goes on in my mind. I am trying to work on living my life, but also on sharing some earthly blessings with you. The feeling of the sun, the wind, the air in my lungs now belongs to you too. I know that 5 or 6 weeks ago, the idea of experiencing life through your mom's body would have been a disgusting thought to you, but I feel now that you possess a different understanding, and if nature, family, and friends are things that you can miss where you are now, to the extent that we are connected, I want to give this gift to you now through the remainder of my life. I will carry you with me always in my heart and you will never be far from my thoughts.

I hope that Ping-Pong kissed you when he arrived on the other side on Saturday. I feel awful that he got so sick before I noticed and did anything about it, and I have vowed to be more attentive going forward.

You are sorely missed here, Aaron. Your friends feel so impacted by your death, and my heart feels like it's been blown to pieces. I don't want you to feel bad about the accident or for causing us this deep sorrow, but instead I want to feel a connection with you, and in so doing, also want to experience some of your peace and joy as well as the connectedness you told Christine you still feel with us. I loved how you said, "It's not like we're never going to see each other again."* So matter of fact and practical, yet living here on earth, we have no certainty about any of those truths. If you are able in any way to help me with any of this, the things I am longing for are: feeling a very certain, everlasting connection to you— one that is filled with peace and love; help with wisdom—how to live a strong and fearless life, filled with love and kindness; and hearing from you from time to time—enough to sustain me.

Enough for now. I love you,
Mom.

(* Used with permission from Christine Sang, Interspecies Communicator. AnimalAwakening.com.)

The reference to Ping-Pong in the letter to Aaron was pertaining to one of our dear cats who became very ill shortly after we lost Aaron. In fact, many animals on the farm became unwell and I strongly believe it was due to the fact that I was exuding such sorrow and grief that it affected every being in my orbit. Jack (horse) became ill, Sam (Aaron's dog) turned up with a lesion on the bridge of her nose, and Ping-Pong's kidney (he had only one) became so infected that his body filled with toxins and it was imperative that we euthanize him to spare him the torture of a slow and painful death.

I blamed myself for not noticing Pingy's distress, but I was so consumed with grief that nothing much got through to me. I can recall mucking stalls and just weeping and sobbing as I shoveled. Being alone in the barn with the horses felt like a safe zone where I could let out the madness that was consuming me. Here again, I was so self-absorbed I didn't realize I would also affect my four-legged family and cause them to become infected with my grief. Or perhaps in their own way, they also felt the loss of Aaron's presence and instead were grieving along with me and not as a result of my sadness. Whichever it was, it was a truly dark time for all of us.

The night we took Ping-Pong to the emergency veterinary clinic, I kissed him and said, "One kiss for you and please give one to Aaron when you see him on the other side." The dear doctor who treated Ping-Pong deserved to know why I said that as we were clinging to our sweet cat. When I explained that my only son had just passed a few weeks prior, that sweet woman just reached for our hands and cried right along with us as we sent our beautiful Ping-Pong to the other side. I'll never forget her deep kindness and authenticity.

I'm ever so grateful for those sweet people that we encounter here on this earth. They seem to turn up at just the right moment and say or do just the thing that provides our torn, haggard souls with a little balm.

I don't think that's an accident.

7/12/2010

Better today, not quite so sad. It probably helped that I felt like I heard from you (in my mind and heart) yesterday.

I think I need to learn to meditate so I can hear you more often. It always happens when I am alone and relatively undistracted.

I felt jealous today when Dan sent me a picture of him and Megan having fun at lunch together.

I wish you were here. I wonder every day what you are doing in your new place and whether you can feel me.

I am afraid about my vision. But I try to tell myself that I can see even without my eyes.

I LOVE YOU ♡

Right before that awful weekend of May 31, I was walking along on the gravel drive by the barn and I noticed the driveway stones appeared very blurry. As we were leaving the very next day for a long weekend at horse camp, I mentioned to Dan that I thought I might need to make an eye appointment when we got back. Little did I know that I was suffering from a sudden onset of macular degeneration, and that I desperately needed a retinologist without delay. As it turned out, I wouldn't see anyone for my eye until weeks and weeks later. After all, I had a funeral for my only son to arrange upon returning from that trip.

I'll never forget sitting in the chair at the eye doctor's office weeks later hearing him murmur those dreaded words:

macular degeneration. I was only 51! How could it be that the condition that claimed both my mother's and father's eyesight, albeit in their late 70s, was affecting me? It felt like someone was heaping burning coals on my head, and that on top of everything else, I now had yet another tragedy to bear. I couldn't even cry. I just sat there like a wooden statue. I had my first eye injection that very day just minutes after the diagnosis. I'd always considered a needle in the eye to be one of my worst nightmares but sat there stoically throughout my treatment.

It wasn't resilience, and it wasn't courage or cowgirl toughness. I was numb. Just plain numb. "What else, God, what else must I endure?" was my only defeated thought. I know now that I was lucky to stumble into this retinologist's world for he's been a solid and stabilizing factor in my life ever since. And I can still see quite well, thank you very much!

Here again, a small gift of care and kindness amidst a maelstrom of suffering and turmoil.

Those early days were very rough.

I hope you don't know what I mean, but I am afraid many of us experience a tremendously significant loss (or losses) in our lifetimes.

Thankfully, Aaron and I were in a good place when he passed out of our time. We didn't always get along. He could be sullen and moody, and there were plenty of times that he just plain didn't like me. But there were many sweet times too. I have a picture of him and me sitting in the sand on the beach at Cape Cod. I had moved away from the rest of the family to sit in a small oasis of shade thrown by the car we had parked on the spit on Chapin Beach. I was enjoying a book when Aaron plopped down next to me. I always felt my heart swell when he wanted to spend time with me. Amazingly, the book I had been reading was, *Many Lives, Many Masters* by Brian Weiss. I knew the book held gravity, but of course had no idea how much more poignant its words would later become, nor how it would make my soul glad years later to see it in my hands in that dear photograph.

The last words on earth that I uttered to Aaron (and he to me) before I left for that horse-camping weekend were, "I love you." A few days before we left, he had come over for dinner, and afterwards Dan encouraged us to go outside while he cleaned up the kitchen. We turned up the music on Aaron's awesome car speakers, got out his lighted Frisbee, and had a wonderful time dancing, laughing, and tossing that Frisbee back and forth in the growing twilight.

It was truly a priceless gift to have that experience as our last earthly time together. It reinforces for me the need to always have the long view—to remember that life can be snatched away in a heartbeat, and that what truly matters, truly matters. Had our last encounter been one where we fought, I'm quite sure I wouldn't even remember what we were angry with each other over, and it certainly wouldn't matter now anyway. Yes, I try to keep the long view in mind now that I'm older, wiser, and have a few scars to show for it.

Do not let the sun go down on your anger.
~Ephesians 4:26

I love this picture of me and Aaron on the beach at Cape Cod. If you were able to see the title of the book I'm reading, it's *Many Lives, Many Masters* by Brian Weiss.

7/16/2010

Things I tell myself to remember:

We are going to see each other again. (But I still want to be your mom!)

We are still connected (It's somewhere near my heart, but it's also soul to soul and mind to mind.)

You don't want me to feel sadness and grief. You want me to be happy, and you don't want to have caused my grief.

You still love me. (And I love you. Always.)

You can send me signs and speak to my mind and heart. (I just need to be still and listen. And I need to learn how to hear my heart.)

You can feel the sun through me. (I need to make sure I pause, give thanks, and send it to you.)

I miss you here on this earthly plane, but I am trying hard to find you and connect with you on the spiritual plane.

God, please don't hurt me anymore.

7/17/2010

Here at our favorite camp in Virginia, we cried hard last night over you. I played the songs from your service, and we talked about how we will never get over losing you.

We said that if humans knew for certain, though, that death was not really an end and that we would be together again, it would really be OK losing someone you loved, and everyone would want to die.

No more Accounting class for you or trying to figure out what kind of a career you'd like.

I wonder if you and Sam communicate easily and often now. By how sweet and loyal she is to me and Dan, I'm choosing to believe 'yes.'

I think that I must choose the things I am going to hold true about your passing because otherwise I will forever be caught in a trap of unending sorrow and grief.

And yes, I grieve about my eye too, but it is nothing compared to the sorrow of missing your physical existence here on this earth.

Today I laid in a lawn chair in the sun and absorbed its rays onto my skin and then offered that feeling to you. That is an example of a good way to think. It honors you and rescues me.

God is not merely a blinding vision of glorious light,
but He is the love that moves the sun and the other stars.
~Dante (*The Divine Comedy*)

We can reach down into the piece of God that resides within all of us (its location is somewhere near the heart, and this is why I think I keep trying to hear my heart and keep getting heart-related messages) and know for sure that not only is He always with us, but that we are all universally connected—just like you said—forever.

I love you; I will never leave you; I will always take care of you is what the God within our heart promises.
No fear is possible then.

In the end, though, maybe we must all give up trying to pay back the people in this world who sustain our lives. In the end, maybe it's wiser to surrender before the miraculous scope of human generosity and to just keep saying thank you, forever and sincerely, for as long as we have voices.
~Elizabeth Gilbert (*Eat Pray Love*)

I happened to pick up Elizabeth Gilbert's *Eat Pray Love* and it felt so providential. Her words uplifted me and offered sustenance when I was weak and my spirit was dark and tormented. Of all the wisdom contained in that book, this resonated the most: "An old Sufi poem says that God long ago drew a circle in the sand exactly around the spot you are standing in now. You were never not coming here. This was never not going to happen."

Reading those words, it hit me; Aaron and I were always going to work off our scripts for this life. We quite possibly agreed to the entire play, not just our own specific scripts. Could soul growth be the purpose? I found a huge measure of comfort in Gilbert's words and the ideas it spawned for me. I hold them true today.

The good stuff and the bad stuff were always going to happen just the way they did—in the past and in our future.
I need to visit you in meditation every day.

People follow different paths, straight or crooked, according to their temperament, depending on which they consider best or most appropriate—and all reach You, just as rivers enter the ocean.
The hub of calmness, that's your heart. That's where God lives within you.
~Elizabeth Gilbert (*Eat Pray Love*)

So, stop looking for answers in the world. Just keep coming back to that center and you'll always find peace.

7/18/2010

The pain was there today, but not so deep and sharp. I told Dan that today I was the happiest I've been since Memorial Day. As we rode along, I thought about you a lot. About your being there with me—riding Lady—like we did last winter that one day. I'm sure glad we had that day together. I love you __so__ much.

Here's a quote I found today that I really like: "Animals are such agreeable friends—they ask no questions; they pass no criticisms."
(George Eliot)

And this one too: "Coincidence is God's way of remaining anonymous."
(Albert Einstein)

7/26/2010

Find him—that connection, ability to talk with him—in my heart. Find my connection to God, the meaning of all this there. Believe that I am still connected to him, can talk to him, hear from him, will see him again.

When you start to lose the battle in your mind, place your mind into your heart, then go into your heart (breathe there), and see what happens.
~Author Unknown

7/27/2010

If I bring forth what's inside me, what's inside me will save me. If I don't bring forth what's inside me, what's inside me will destroy me.
~Jesus (*Gnostic Gospel of Thomas*)

When a child is killed, two people really die. The only difference is that his mother still must suffer a heartbeat.

7/31/10 - Equinection

Several weeks ago, I made plans to visit Equinection, a beautiful farm situated on 100+ acres in the mountains of

North Carolina. Dan and I had been there a couple of years prior for a private session with the owner and founder, Karen, and my heart tugged at my mind to make arrangements to go there once again—this time by myself. I had felt deeply connected to the land the first time we visited Equinection. I can remember whispering to Dan after passing through the gates and as we rounded the bend to view the sweeping vista of the immaculate grounds, "I feel like I've been here before; like I have lived here." Something was pulling me back, but this time my hope was that I could be lifted from the mire of despair that hung over and oppressed me. Those heart tugs turned out to be right, and I'm so glad I went. The following is the unaltered version of my time spent there, alone with Karen and my equine partner:

Saturday, 10 a.m.

Romeo was in the middle stall when I arrived. Just like last time, I was drawn to him. His majesty, power, and size; curved neck, soft brown eyes, and big feathery feet.

Karen and I walked. I told her about Aaron, and I cried a lot. A filly came down from a hilly pasture to look at me and stand by me. Karen told me she'd been abandoned and was starving. Yet she doesn't begrudge any of the horses around her now their share of grass and she has accepted her surroundings here just like she simply accepted her previous circumstances. Her heart is pure. And it is open.

I told Karen you visited me a few nights ago in a dream and told me that I'd done a good job with you, and I think you also said you loved me. Karen said a visitation is always positive in this way. I believe you and I believe what you said.

When I told her about the first thoughts that came to me when I heard the awful news that you had died—that you are at peace and you are safe— she said that was God speaking to me and that it is true. When I told her

25

that Rodney Crowell's song: "Till I Can Gain Control Again" came into my mind when I learned of your death, she said that those words were also from God and that they were a very powerful and important message to me: "Out on the road that lies before me now, there are some turns where I will spin. I only hope that you will hold me now. Till I can gain control again." She mentioned being alone, and I also shared with her these words from that same song: "Just like a lighthouse you must stand alone. Landmark a sailor's journey's end. No matter what seas I've been sailing on, I'll always pass this way again." She says these words are incredibly significant.

We then rounded the bend in the path up by the big teapot sculpture that sat on a hill in the meadow, and she asked me to stop and close my eyes and feel my body starting with the head and moving down to my feet. As she was guiding me, she asked me to tell her what I saw. I told her there was an eye. It was the yellow eye of a wolf. She became very excited and told me about the symbolism of the wolf in the Cherokee culture—ground we were standing on. The wolf is independent, strong, and a very spiritual animal to the Indians. He is found at all four points of the compass. I have the strength, power, and independence of the wolf spirit.

She then pointed out a black mare (that looked a lot like Lady) standing and eating in an orchard. She said to go as close as I wanted and stand there with my back to her. I closed my eyes and talked about how I was feeling. From 15 yards away where she'd been happily eating grass, Willow walked over to my side, nuzzled my arm near my mid-section and heart, and then gently reached up to my head where she pushed and then gently bit at my temple. To Karen, this signified me needing to get something out of my head and find some answers being in my heart— exactly what I had felt I was needing to do and why I'd come.

We then moved on and began working on an exercise that was very difficult for me. It entailed marking a line that represented today, and then walking back in time through my life to try to find the root of the doubt and fear that has me so caught in a rut when I try to reconcile with your death.

It was very difficult for me to identify my feelings and thoughts during this exercise, but the points that came up as I walked backwards were: your death and my grief over that; when I was 31 years old living on Charter Street, standing on the wood floors in the living room while you slept in your crib, but feeling like I had so much to do; then when I was 17 and changing from being carefree and happy-go-lucky to being responsible and really ruled by my ideology; then when I was in third grade and how mean Sister Rosatina was, but yet I was unsupported by my parents; to first grade when I was scared of all the new kids I was meeting, when I peed in front of the whole class, and how terrified I was of the loud bathrooms; then finally to me as a baby in nothing but a diaper, laying in something in the kitchen alone. The feeling of being alone, unsupported, and having to fend for myself which led to a lifetime of fear and doubt. I then walked further back and found a time that was free, peaceful, and calm—and without fear. When she asked me at the end of the exercise whether I wanted to walk back to the present or stay in the time before I was born, I wanted to stay in the latter.

At the end of the exercise as we were walking back to the barn, a spotted horse from a pasture up the hill aligned directly with me. (I recall that he even lifted one of his front legs in a very regal way.) Karen asked me to observe him and tell her what it meant.
He was so proud, full of himself, and strong.

The exercise was exhausting to me, so we took a break.

When I returned, Romeo was waiting for me in the covered arena. Karen and I sat in chairs in the middle of the arena, and I shared my mandala with her—the picture that I had drawn of the walking back in time experience. As I did so, my tears began to fall. She told me to go into the feeling and as I sat there with my eyes closed sobbing, Romeo walked over. This is the horse that last time Dan and I were here, I was drawn to. I had drawn a picture of him and I told Karen that he symbolized the heart to me. So today as I was sitting there crying, this magnificent horse walked to me, stood over me with his heart very near my head, and as I leaned my head onto his shoulder, I looked up and he was shedding tears from his

27

right eye. *He was grieving with me. Throughout the next hour, he remained positioned over me, often touching my head or my heart with his nose. When I stopped crying, he would stop crying. When I started up again, so did he. I watched as his tears fell to the sand on the arena floor along with mine. Time and again he positioned himself in between me and Karen—almost as if to say, "Let me do the work; I'll take over."*

Karen began exploring something I'd talked about earlier—my relationship many years ago with Wayne and how I thought that tied in to you. And there we were in this giant enclosed arena with a single car garage door type entrance when I saw a giant black butterfly come in and fly high above us in this enormous tent-like structure. I told Karen the story about my deceased mom and how I believed—or wanted to believe that she embodied butterflies. As we talked more about the relationship with Wayne and its outcome—this butterfly flew down to the floor of the arena, fluttered near Karen's legs, flew under Romeo, and fluttered under his legs. Karen was certain it was my mom, doing what a shaman does to take away the hurt and guilt and that she was releasing me, forgiving me, and helping me get rid of the guilt over feeling as though I had rejected you. That giant black butterfly then left and Karen helped me to speak to that spirit that Wayne and I had produced, and it wasn't you after all. All I could see was purity and with my eyes closed, I could see Romeo and the purity of his heart and that's it. No guilt, no shame, nothing to do with you.

Karen explained that Romeo was a reflection of me. And when all of this came out about Wayne and you—or really not you—Romeo yawned repeatedly right over my lap, and he was literally spewing junk out of his mouth. Karen said he was getting rid of all the garbage—exactly what was happening with me.

After that Romeo spent a lot of time blocking me from the doorway that I started out the exercise in—the 51-year-old full of doubt and fear, and pointing me to the before—the past where there was peace and calm and safety.

Karen then left me alone with Romeo and he seemed to indicate I should follow him back into that place of peace and calm. He came back once again to yawn and release and affirm our work.

I am exhausted—back at it again tomorrow at 9:30.

I sleep alone tonight in a cabin under a picture of a wolf at Yellowstone.

8/1/2010

Arrived at 9:30. We walked to a lower pasture where there were two black horses and next to their area, a fire ring. A fire was lit in the ring.

*As we approached this area, Karen asked me to stop and look at the horses and tell her what I knew about them. I started to say they were mares, but I second guessed myself and said nothing was coming to me. She then asked me to choose a place near the horses to stand quietly and go into my heart to see what I would learn. So, I chose a spot, stood there quietly, and tried to listen to my feelings and my heart. After quite a while, I crouched down and I began to feel that I had been there before. Crouched down in that manner I saw a young Indian—maybe 18 or 19 years old. He (me) was alone and felt very strong and vital—full of confidence and at one with the earth.
Certain of his place and purpose.*

*As I crouched there with my eyes closed thinking about this time before, I heard shuffling in the grass and the large dark horse had come over to me. A confirmation of the authenticity of my thoughts. I touched her nose, and after a moment, she walked a few paces away and began eating. I returned to my thoughts of the Indian boy—me—and while in this space, I once again heard a shuffling in the grass. The smaller horse had come to me. Again, making certain that I had confirmation that my thoughts and visions were true. I touched this horse's nose and she too soon walked off.
And of course, during their visits I confirmed what I knew from a distance but was too doubtful to say; that they were indeed mares. Later in*

our conversation when I told this to Karen, she told me to stop the doubt and go with my first feeling.

So, I then walked back over to Karen who, not surprisingly, had prepared an Indian smoke ceremony for me. It's called a smudging ceremony and she burned sage to perform it over me. It felt very right in that old place where we stood—where I felt I had lived before as an Indian boy—to receive the smoke ceremony.

We then went to the bench near the smoke ring where the fire was burning and began to talk. We talked a lot about Aaron—his love of nature, and when I finally told her about the Indian boy, she said it was the truth. One comment Karen made was, "There is nothing about you that looks like a 51-year-old woman." This as we were discussing the Indian's muscles, bones, and strong lungs. And as we were discussing it, and how I should not doubt what my heart tells me, she began to tell me about three birds that visited while I was having my vision of the Indian boy. As she was explaining, suddenly a very large butterfly flew directly in between us and as I was exclaiming how incredible it was that my mom showed up while we were discussing the validity of what I learned, a beautiful black and teal blue dragonfly flew into our midst—along with the butterfly— and lit briefly on my knee. I told Karen about our thoughts that the dragonfly was you, Aaron, and she of course already knew that was the truth too. I closed my eyes in thankfulness, wonder, and to shed a few tears over the power of what had just happened, and while my eyes were closed, a very loud buzz with a soft whoosh of air went by my right ear. I instantly opened my eyes, looked at Karen and said, "What was that?" Before she responded, I knew it had been the dragonfly—you—in our midst. Once again confirming the truth, our always connection, and the two-way nature of our connection.

Karen then went on to explain the three birds that had come while I was with the Indian:

Woodpecker: connection to the earth; ability to find hidden layers; understands rhythms, cycles, and patterns; pecks away at deception until the truth is revealed.

Red-tailed hawk: who flies lower than the eagle and hunts his prey with his eyes. And he can find a small vole from very high in the sky because his vision is so acute. This is unlike the eagle who hunts by instinct and not by sight.

The crows: symbols of universal justice and also humor. (There were many crows, a couple of woodpeckers, and one red-tailed hawk that visited.)

Karen also asked me to take a piece of paper and using my left hand, to have the Indian write to me or me to write to the Indian. The following words came tumbling out:

Alone, but strong

With the earth

The smoke

You've done this all before

Don't be afraid

I am with you

Aaron is in your right arm now

You know the butterfly

And you don't need your eyes to see*

I am strong with the earth

You know me.

*Somewhere around where the asterisks lie in the above, Karen said to me to unclench my right hand. I laughed because I had written that that was Aaron in my right hand before she even said it.

Before we stopped our session in that very old place—where I had once lived—I burned my own sage in the fire and said blessings for that place.

We walked back to the barn where Romeo and I said our goodbyes. Karen had turned him loose, and at liberty, he came to find me and before we parted, he nickered to me and I came to him as he stood waiting for me, and we gently put our heads together in a final exchange of our heart connection and thought connection.

My takeaways from all this:

Like the wolf—alone, independent, self-sufficient, an old Indian symbol.

Like the spotted horse—sure, vital, and strong.

Like the Indian—a body that is strong, lean, and young.

That to know truth, breathe deep, go into my heart and listen to what is there. The first images are true. Animals confirm this for us.

Aaron and I are connected. He is everywhere around me, and I can reach him just as easily as he can reach me.

That there is no right, wrong, or injustice about what happened. That it just is. Just like everything just is. And that everything always was and always will be.

We know the truth inside us.

That when you set your intentions, things begin to start shaping for them to unfold.

That the feelings of grief and sorrow are true and are good to express.

That Aaron is who he is and I am who I am. That I didn't create his spirit or even his body. It took God to do that.

And after I arrived back home, that Sammie was also the Indian boy's mongrel dog, and there was a deep bond between them.

Peace…

Truth is within ourselves, it takes no rise from outward things,
whatever you may believe.
There is an inmost center in us all, where truth abides in
fullness; and around, wall upon wall, the gross flesh hems it in,
this perfect, clear perception—which is truth.
A baffling and perverting carnal mash binds it and makes all
error: and to know rather consists in opening out a way
whence the imprisoned splendor may escape,
than in effecting entry for a light supposed to be without.
~Robert Browning (*Paracelsus*)

8/5/2010

From Karen who reminds me that: I connected to Aaron, to know him in my heart. I connected to him through my heart and by the way of awareness of the moment.
The grief I am experiencing is sacred. It is a mother's grief that transforms me into a grounded and whole being.
Romeo (Ceili) brought this message to me—my grief is sacred. I won't be

grieving my whole life, but through the grief I will find my way to higher consciousness. The changes that I have made will stay with me, I can trust myself.

Ask the very beasts, and they will teach you; ask the wild birds, they will tell you; crawling creatures will instruct you, fish in the sea will inform you. For which of them all know not that this is the Eternal's way, in whose control lies every living soul, and the whole life of man.
~Job 12:7-10

There are invisible bridges for friendly and helpful two-way communication or thought traffic. Mental bridges extending from where we are functioning as intelligent expressions of life to where animals are also doing the same. Intuitive bridges, built upon that speech which does not have to be uttered, across which we and animals can freely send and receive and share. Heart bridges by means of which we can constantly adjust ourselves to them rather than demanding they adjust ourselves to us.
~A.J. Boone (*Kinship With All Life*)

Just like what Karen said last weekend about communicating not only with the animals, but now with Aaron.

Impressions will come to me as gently as the breath of a light whisper.

Thou shalt also decree a thing, and it shall be established unto
thee:
and the light shall shine upon thy ways.
~Job 22:28

*With the accuracy and precision of an echo, we get back in outward
experience just what we are mentally and vocally decreeing and expecting.*

I expect:

To continue to hear from and to connect to Aaron

My eye to improve

The things I learned this weekend to stay with me

(To) arrive at a higher consciousness

To know and be able to better communicate with animals

To be led to a satisfying life path

*To see and experience Aaron again both physically one day and mentally
and spiritually until then*

(To) continue to grow in love and in my relationship with Dan

8/17/2010

This is hard, but not hopeless. Things I believe:

Aaron is still living

He is very near me

I will see him again

This is part of my spiritual journey—one that I chose

This life is temporary

I must go on and continue to learn and grow in my journey

There is nothing to fear

There is no hell

Aaron likes me to pray for him and talk to him

He would like me to make a memorial for him

The pain of this loss will temper the rest of my existence here. I can either fall down with the weight of my grief or I can learn to carry it as I go on with my journey.
~George Anderson (*Lessons From The Light*)

8/27/2010

Everyone talks about the heart when it comes to you, my love.

I miss you so, want you back, and love you so very much.

Come to me in my dreams again soon—and please keep whispering in my ear.

You were a wonder to me when you were born, and you are and always will be one of the greatest loves of my heart.

I look forward to seeing you again.

Please meet me at the gate.

Sam is well.

Blood is in the heart.
~Matthew Cross

8/31/2010

*Summer's almost over, and it's been three months since that awful
Memorial Day.
I have been busy with work and school, but you are ever present, if only
on the fringes of my thoughts.*

*You are with me at all times—I carry you in my heart and in my soul. I
love you and will love you until the end of time.*

*Today I picked up your gray winter hat and breathed in the scent of you. I
will never let anyone put that hat on because I want to always be able to
smell the essence of you—no matter how faint the years may dim your
smell.*

I love you, my son. Always and forever.

When God created the horse, He said to the magnificent
creature: I have made thee as no other. All the treasures of the
earth shall lie between thy eyes. Thou shalt cast thy enemies
between thy hooves, but thou shalt carry my friends upon thy

back. Thy saddle shall be the seat of prayers to me. And thou
fly without any wings and conquer without any sword.
Oh, horse.
~The Koran

9/9/2010

I've been a lifelong reader, and there were many quotes in
various materials I was reading that were really resonating
with me. On those days, I merely recorded other author's
thoughts. I'm sure it's because they mirrored so much of what
I was experiencing, and they provided me with a deep
measure of truth and comfort. Here are excerpts that I found
deeply meaningful—try to slow down and take some time to
absorb and savor these words:

Spiritual traditions since the beginning of time have taught
that it is through the eternal nature of our souls that we
develop the capacity to tolerate, endure, and even peacefully
accept conflict, contradictions, incompatibilities, and dualities.
As our spiritual perceptions mature in these ways, we open
ourselves to a reality beyond polarities and dualities, to an
underlying unity. Within that unity our souls expand. We open
up to a greater tolerance for dissonance and an acceptance of
contradiction. We do so not through martyrdom or
masochism, but by living peacefully with that which we cannot
resolve. Learning to live intimately with life's contradictions
helps us gather energy wherein, ironically, our creativity swells.
The ever-moving energy of the soul nurtures us toward
wholeness until we at last learn to see and accept incongruity
in the world, ourselves, and other creatures. From this ability
we gain inner harmony even in the midst of inner and outer

chaos. We drop illusion and fantasy, and like an eagle, begin to see the bigger picture with exceptional clarity.

In time, seeing what is real, even when it is upsetting, will not shake our inner core. We observe what is—beauty or darkness —without turmoil. As we view ourselves from the vantage point of the soul,

We learn patience with ourselves and others, and from this acquire the inner strength to abide psychological pain.

The inward journey requires us to radically shift our perceptions and attitudes—to stop thinking things must go our way or as planned, and to acknowledge imperfections in ourselves and others without rage, hatred, prejudice, or intolerance. Following this path, we uproot our assumptions and preconceived ideas. We become exposed and able to love.

As we continue to travel on the inward journey, we develop intuitive radar. We can gain the ability to know all is well even in the midst of tragedy, for then we truly begin to identify ourselves with a greater reality.

Our experience extends far beyond our normal sensory perceptions and mental process. We discover and cultivate a different kind of mind and heart, one that accesses truth rather than invents it.

Once activated, the mystical mind and heart hunger to resume a relationship that has been interrupted—the torrid and timeless love affair between God and the soul. While we have all known this relationship before, our memory of it, in most cases, is suppressed soon after birth.

~Adele von Rüst McCormick, Marlena Deborah McCormick, and Thomas E. McCormick. (*Horses and the Mystical Path*. Copyright© 2004. Reprinted with permission by New World Library, Novato, CA. www.newworldlibrary.com.)

9/20/2010

Dear Aaron:

We watched Alice in Wonderland last night. I remember when you were going to see it with your friends. I think you arranged to meet them late one night at Piper Glen for the show. As I recall, you really weren't that impressed with it, but I actually really liked it. My very favorite part was when Absalom, the blue caterpillar, said as he was turning into a cocoon, "I hope to see you again in another life."

I know you know why I liked that line.

We come into this world with a biological and psychological need to survive. As a result, we initially adhere to a simple rule: first things first. As we focus our attention on the maintenance of our physical beings, our memories of soul and God fade. This healthy and necessary amnesia continues until we can learn to love without losing our minds and shucking worldly responsibilities. Meanwhile, our survival—both physical and psychological—becomes dependent upon that portion of our beings that we call ego. Through our submission to the ego, we not only lose sight of our relationship with God, but develop a whole new set of perceptions dedicated to our welfare in the physical world.
~Adele von Rüst McCormick, Marlena Deborah McCormick, and Thomas E. McCormick. (*Horses and the Mystical Path.* Copyright© 2004. Reprinted with permission by New World Library, Novato, CA. www.newworldlibrary.com.)

9/22/2010

There's a saying in the valley (Napa)—the grapes like to suffer.
Grapes overwatered and babied do not develop as intense a
flavor as those that have struggled.
Live according to nature, following the rhythm of its seasons,
births, disasters, and death, and experience firsthand the age-
old dictum of life as an unbroken circle.
~Adele von Rüst McCormick, Marlena Deborah
McCormick, and Thomas E. McCormick. (*Horses and the
Mystical Path*. Copyright© 2004. Reprinted with permission by
New World Library, Novato, CA. www.newworldlibrary.com.)

9/30/2010

*I can't believe summer's over. It began so horribly, and now it feels like it
just slipped away.*

*You've been playing a lot of pranks on me lately. The cell phone, locking
my keys in the truck, and the loud alarm clock at the hotel yesterday.*

*I'm glad you're turning up in my dreams too, although I'd love a
visitation.
I am missing you so.*

*Sam is happy. You would think she is fat, though. I bought her some diet
food. ☺ (First smile since this journal began. I think you know I need the
lighthearted pranks more than what I think I need from you. I like
thinking of you as a wise man. Let's be friends. You'd like me better. ☺
Smile again.*

Of the pranks listed above, the only one I remember clearly is
the incident with the cell phone. I had gone to New York to
visit clients—my first trip since your accident. It was tough
and emotional, but it felt good to be supported and embraced

by my work family and it felt good to be doing 'normal' things again.

On the way back, our plane was delayed on the tarmac, and I remember using my cell phone to call home and let Dan know I was going to be late. I placed the phone in the seat pocket in front of me and sank back into the seat for what I hoped would be a nap for my weary mind and body. As I drifted into sleep, I remember thinking that I should retrieve the phone out of the seat pocket and put it into my bag to ensure I didn't leave it on the plane. Too tired to move, I sank into rest.

When we landed, I exited the plane and took the shuttle bus to my parking lot. As I sank down in the driver's seat of my car, I reached in my bag for my phone to make my customary call Dan to let him know I was enroute. I remember my alarm upon discovering the phone was not in my bag. I raced back to the terminal and when I got out, I thoroughly searched my seat, under the seat, and all around the floors and other seats in the car, but to no avail. I dashed back out to the gate where my plane was just getting ready to leave for its next journey. The ticket agent listened to my story, and despite the jetway door being closed, she called someone on board and told me the flight attendant would look in my seat pocket before the plane pulled out.

After what seemed like an eternity, the phone rang at the agent's desk. The flight attendant reported searching not only my seat pocket, but the seats, floor, and entire row in front and in back of where I'd sat. Unfortunately, no phone was found. My heart sank as the gate agent gave me the news. Tears sprang as my heart broke. The kind agent said, "I know, so much of our lives are tied to our cell phones now." I replied, "It's more than that. You see, my son died in a car accident on May 31, and my one and only text message from him just six days prior to his accident is on that phone." Texting being a new thing at the time was something I had never done. But on that day, May 25, I had reached out to Aaron by text with a simple, "How are you?" He had written right back telling me, "Good, I'll call you here in a little bit." That simple text was a living link to what had been, and I was devastated to think I'd never see it again.

My sadness was so palpable that the gate agent began to cry too, and assured me that if anyone found it, they'd turn it in and the airline would give it back. She urged me to go directly to Lost & Found and make a claim. I remember feeling like I was made out of rubber as I walked to the office to file that claim.

When I got back to my car, I unlocked the passenger side door and dumped my entire purse out on the seat. As I was rummaging through the various contents of my purse, I felt almost as if a finger touched my chin and lifted my head up. As my eyes followed the motion of my head, I saw the steering wheel, and then, there on the driver's seat, my phone.

Right there in the middle of the seat in plain sight sat the phone that I had left in the seat pocket of the airplane. I stood there with my jaw dropped in stunned amazement that my phone had been returned to me. No one could have placed it there while I was in the terminal as I had locked the doors. And besides that, no one would have known to return the missing phone to that specific car. Had the phone been on my seat all along, I certainly would have felt it when I sat down. Had I dropped it there, I would have seen it when I performed my first search before going back to the gate or for sure when I performed my second search when I got back to the terminal. No, somehow in this universe, it had been returned to me. Maybe an angel, maybe Aaron. I'll never know for sure, but it was a miracle.

Although I no longer use that old flip phone, I occasionally plug it in and have a look at that precious text and I'm reminded of the power that exists beyond the realm of our sight and our so-called physical, earthly limitations. I'm grateful for the kindness of other humans, and I'm grateful for miracles.

Experiences igniting revelation and epiphany often come at
the most unexpected and even mundane moments in our lives.
And yet, in their own way they affirm our connections with
the Divine. In these moments, we are reminded that the
material plane is not the main show, but only a fragment of a
much larger reality.

As they strolled, he spoke about hermeticism—the study of
the unseen dimensions of reality—and humanity.

All healing comes from the spirit. If you wish to know God,
you must immerse yourselves in nature, spend hours
contemplating a flower or an animal. Your heart will open to
the unseen world.

As a student of human nature, you already know many of
these things. Keep going. Go deeper. The whole of reality is
invisible, and those of us who know it are connected in a
cosmic brotherhood. We always recognize each other.

~Adele von Rüst McCormick, Marlena Deborah
McCormick, and Thomas E. McCormick. (*Horses and the
Mystical Path*. Copyright© 2004. Reprinted with permission by
New World Library, Novato, CA. www.newworldlibrary.com.)

Between my experiences at Equinection as well as the various
pranks and impossible things that were happening all around
me, I was beginning to understand that we really do have a
connection to a stronger, eternal force that lies just outside of
our physical grasp, but is pressing on us and trying to impress
upon us nonetheless. And I was discovering many others knew
it and were aware of it, but were almost afraid to talk about it,
perhaps fearing the disbelief or pity of others. Now if only I
could grasp it, hang on to it, and live my remaining life coda
by it. Essentially, unlearning all the 'black and white' stuff
we're all taught about how the world works, and remembering

what we knew at our core when we entered this world. It's not easy, but it is enlightening, and it brings peace, comfort, and hope to a grieving heart.

11/1/2010

I had a visitation from you last week. Just you standing there with your white t-shirt on and your hair slightly longer than you'd been wearing it. You didn't say anything, but your face was open and you looked so good.

Then last night, I talked to you a lot and cried before I went to sleep. I was thinking about how it was very likely that time passes very slowly for you now and that that's why it seems so infrequent that I see you in my dreams or hear from you in other ways. So, I asked you to show me some signs that you were OK and happy, and I had a dream about you. You were a little boy again and it had something to do with a white lizard. We were cleaning the lizard, and everything between you and me was just great. I can't recall much more now other than that, but it was really good.

When Aaron was a little boy, our dog, Jet, caught a lizard and had mangled him up pretty badly by the time I noticed and wrestled it out of his mouth. Aaron, ever nearby his mom when we were outside, asked if we could try to save him. I was pretty sure it was going to be an exercise in disappointment and heartache, but nonetheless I agreed we could try.

We stationed the lizard in a little empty aquarium we had and filled it with soft grass and pine needles. We added some sticks for climbing (which the lizard was very incapable of at that moment), and a little dish of water. We kept him outside on the porch where he could enjoy some sunshine in what I felt was a rapidly waning existence.

Later that day, we brought him some things to eat— lettuce, fruit, and things we imagined a little lizard might like. We covered his aquarium with a towel for the night and I felt sure we'd find a stiff lizard in there the next morning. After

45

breakfast, Aaron remembered the little guy and we went outside to check on him. I was ready to have the conversation about death, however, to my surprise, the little fellow was bright eyed, and we could see he'd eaten some of the things we'd left for him.

He remained with us for several days while he recuperated, and when we deemed it safe for him to go back to living independently, we released him (and made sure Jet was confined to the house). Without so much as a backward glance, our lizard took up his old life. I remember Aaron and me smiling and discussing how well we'd done, and I congratulated him for having had such a good idea. That little incident taught us a lot about love, care, and hope. Perhaps that's where the lizard from my dream emanated.

11/2/2010

I feel tired.

Old.

Beat down.

Sometimes I don't care if I live or die. I have very little fear anymore.

I try to think of my truisms, but I still shed tears every day.

Why did you have to leave?

Why did I ever sign up for this?

Will it ever stop hurting so bad?

Will I ever really know why?

I was finding that in one day's time I could vacillate between feeling strong and encouraged to feeling utterly low and full of despair. The times of strength and encouragement felt like small oases of mercy. The times of despair felt like thorns raking my entire being. I plodded along enduring, learning, and sometimes feeling a small breeze of relief.

11/5/2010

I'm not sure why I wrote another journal entry about the lizard just a few days after the first time I talked about it, but I like this entry a lot:

You popped up in my dreams the other night. You were a little boy again and you had a white lizard that I was helping you clean. Do you remember the lizard that Jet just about killed and you asked me if we could make a hospital for him so we could try to save him? We did, and I was very worried he'd die on us, but we prayed for him, gave him food and water, and talked to him. And wouldn't you know it, after a couple days he started perking up, and would regard us with his reptilian eyes and little cocked head.

We rejoiced when we were able to set him free to resume his lizard life.

Tell him hello and thank you from me, if he's there with you now—I know their life spans are short.

You also visited me a few nights ago. You were wearing a white T-shirt and had your longer haircut. You didn't say anything, but you looked so good to me.

I've felt your presence a lot over the last couple of days while I'm in NJ for a Tony Robbins seminar. I think you were sitting next to me on the plane, and you've warmed me or bathed me in light a couple times at the seminar. This has been difficult; very draining for me, but someone, an earth angel I met today, told me you and I had a spiritual contract. I liked that thought a lot and it has helped me already, a great deal. Worth coming here if I walk away with nothing else.

11/19/2010

We're here at our mountain cabin, and you would love it. There's a big deck, facing west, with a beautiful view of the sun setting behind the mountains. Peter said it's "epic" and the best cabin ever. I tried for that every year—something that would really please you guys and where we would create memories. It seems so weird to be here without you. I know you're here with us in spirit, and we are dedicating this weekend to you tonight in a smudge ceremony.

As I looked out over the mountains, I imagined you there, triumphant from a long, hard climb. I was reminded of that song, "Just like the sun over the mountaintop, you know I'll always come again..." Come back soon my son, and in the meantime stay ever close in spirit. I love you now and forever.

There is an unseen world all around us. What we see here is only a fragment of a larger reality.

I'm no longer on a physical journey with Aaron, but a spiritual journey. I know all is well despite tragedy because we are all part of a greater reality.

When I wrote the above entry in my journal, I was reminded of our annual pre-Thanksgiving mountain cabin weekend from the previous year. Aaron, Matthew, Peter, and Lincoln decided to drive to a mountain in the distance—one that we could see from our cabin window—and leave the car at the bottom and walk to the top.

Several hours after the boys left the cabin, my phone rang. Aaron excitedly told me he was at the top and told me to look out the window because he was waving to me. I immediately went to the window, but of course I couldn't see him as he was at least three miles away. He said he was jumping up and down and waving his arms and that I should look really hard. I remember wishing I could see him, but confessing that no, I couldn't. He asked if I could see the large metal tower on the mountain. That I could see. He was delighted to tell me he was standing next to it, and I assured him I felt like we could almost see one another now that I knew right where he was standing.

After he passed, I remember thinking that it's kind of like that now. He's there. Just out of my sight, just out of my reach, but there, nonetheless. I love remembering that day he called me from that mountain. I love that in his excitement he cared to call me. I ask him now to give me a call all the time. And I do get a lot of little nudges from him. Especially if I'm listening with my heart.

Indeed, the fate of man and beast is identical; one dies, the
other too, and both have the same breath; man has no
advantage over the beast, for all is vanity. Both go to the same
place; both originate from the dust and to the dust both
return. Who knows if the spirit of man mounts upward or if
the spirit of the beast goes down to the earth?
~Ecclesiastes 3:19 (*The Jerusalem Bible*)

The only place our individual minds and the Divine mind can
meld is in our hearts. Since our heart of hearts belongs to
God, it is a private and silent rendezvous. Communion is an
unceasing prayer of the heart, and our only transport into this
unseen world. We travel to this invisible place in silence,
reminiscent of our non-verbal beginnings. Momentarily we
cease our excessive dependency on meaningless and empty
words.
~Adele von Rüst McCormick, Marlena Deborah
McCormick, and Thomas E. McCormick. (*Horses and the
Mystical Path.* Copyright© 2004. Reprinted with permission by
New World Library, Novato, CA. www.newworldlibrary.com.)

11/24/2010

Deep peace to you
Deep peace of the flowing air to you
Deep peace of the deep sea to you
Deep peace of the night to you
Moon and stars pour light on you
~William Sharp (Adapted from *The Dominion of Dreams Under a
Dark Star*)

12/14/2010

Man is created in God's image.

*If God is everlasting, and we have been created in His image, then so are
we. Aaron lives. I will see him again one day. Why is this so difficult of
a truth to hold on to when most of us know it innately?*

A famous Hermetic aphorism says, "Know ye not that ye are gods?"

"As above, so below." Man created in God's image…Apotheosis.

*This persistent message of man's own divinity—of his hidden potential
—was the recurring theme in the ancient texts of countless traditions.
Even the Bible cried out in Psalms 82:6, "Ye are Gods!"*

*Many of us live trapped between two worlds—one foot in the spiritual,
one foot in the physical. Your heart yearns to believe, but your intellect
fights to permit it.*

*Einstein said, "That which is impenetrable to us really exists. Behind the
secrets of nature remains something subtle, intangible, and inexplicable.
Veneration for this force beyond anything that we can comprehend
is my religion."*

*Jesus taught that the kingdom of God is within you. He even promised us,
"The works I do, you can do…and greater."*
~John 14:12.

Abandon the search for God…instead, take yourself as a starting place.

*Our minds can generate energy capable of transforming physical matter.
Particles react to our thoughts which means our thoughts have the power to
change the world.*

The kingdom of God is within you.
~Luke 17:20

Chaos Theory tells us that even small variations of (or minor changes to) the initial condition of a dynamic system may produce large variations in the long-term behavior (or outcome) of the system. Commonly called The Butterfly Effect, the idea is illustrated elegantly by the thought that something as gentle as the fluttering of a butterfly's wings can cause a typhoon halfway around the world.

In other words, everything affects everything. Our very thoughts are energy. And as I stated all those years ago in my journal, our thoughts have the power to change the world.

1/3/2011

It was a new year, and in only a few months, it was going to be one year since we'd lost you. There were so many firsts without you and more yet to come. I didn't want to think about your 21st birthday coming up in March nor the first anniversary of your passing. It felt on that very first day like every minute and hour that ticked by took me further and further away from you. I hated that time just marched on when all I wanted was for it to have stood still prior to May 31, 2010.

At Christmas we all sat in the living room opening gifts and I wondered if the rest of the family was also feeling the sadness and emptiness of a room filled with everyone but you. I was crying softly to myself when Dan said, "Mary, look up, I want to take your picture." Clearly, I was the only one crying and no one else had even realized I was on an island of despair all by myself in that crowded, noisy room. I wiped my cheeks and tried to smile for the picture, but I looked like hell. I guess it's a good thing that we all don't feel exactly the same way as one another, otherwise what a bunch of lousy sad sacks would have filled our room that day and what a gloomy and dreary Christmas it would have been!

Over the holiday, we watched one of the Narnia movies, _Voyage of the Dawn Treader_, and I loved the scene where Lucy and Aslan had this exchange:

"Is there a way to Aslan's country from our world?

There is a way into my country from all worlds, said Aslan.

Will you tell us how to get into your country from our world?

I shall be telling you all the time. But I will not tell you how long or short the way will be; only that it lies across a river. But do not fear that, for I am the great Bridge Builder."
~C.S. Lewis

I feel like Aaron is in Aslan's country.

2/1/2011

I had a dream a couple of weeks ago in which Aaron appeared before me and seemed very, very real and physically present. I asked him how he was able to do this, and he said, "I'm really not supposed to, but I knew you needed it."

It made me feel very connected and close to him and made me less doubtful. I am still always longing for more, but it's a blessing in a sea of grief and heartache.

We moved to our new house on January 20th, and we both really feel comfortable here. It's a warm and earthy home, and a place where I feel very connected to Aaron.

Aaron's car accident took place on our road, only a couple of miles from our house. I hated driving by the tree he slammed into nearly every day, and yet, I had no stamina for putting the house on the market, finding or building a new one, and packing up and moving. Fate intervened, and a couple called us wondering if we would be interested in selling our house to them. I told Dan that the very thought exhausted me, but that at the same time, I wanted very much to not have to drive past the scene of his death multiple times a week either. Dan being Dan, he came up with the perfect solution: we would sell the house, but we would rent back from the couple while we were building our new home. We found a lovely piece of property only 15 minutes away and Dan built our second subdivision with us situated on ten acres in the cul de sac smack in the middle of a beautiful woods. It was peaceful and serene, and all the animals also loved it there. Now we drive past the scene of the accident only if we are deliberately intending to visit it.

2/10/2011

Today I'm reminded of this verse from Psalm 34:18: "The Lord is close to the brokenhearted."

2/16/2011

I missed you a lot on Valentine's Day. I remembered how every year I would ask you if you would be my Valentine and you'd consider briefly, and then answer seriously, "Yes."

Remember how I always wanted you to have a tattoo that said "I Love Mom" and you always wanted me to draw an eagle instead, that you could have tattooed somewhere?

My compromise was to suggest an eagle holding a banner in his talons that says,
"I Love Mom."

I don't really like tattoos—they're too permanent to suit me—and I never really wanted Aaron to get one, but if he was hell-bent on it, I always wanted it to be one that professed his love for me! I was pleased that he wanted it to be one of my raptor drawings, so I thought the banner in the talons was a great idea. We laughed about that, Aaron and I.

This is one of my sketches of a Red-Tailed Hawk
that Aaron always liked.

2/22/2011

*Had another dream about you last night. In this dream you were young—
maybe only eight or nine years old. I was somehow either traveling back in
time or had some pre-awareness of your death because I remember picking
you up or holding you very close and breathing in your smell and feeling
your skin on mine and I was thinking I would warn you not to come over
on the eve of Memorial Day for the party, but then I thought I would
surely see you and be with you again and I should wait until you were a
little older to tell you.*

*So, in this dream I was aware of now, but was somehow transported
back in time—or you were transported to now, but as a little boy. It all
seemed so real that when I woke up, I really wondered if there was some
way that I or you couldn't go back in time so as to accommodate this
warning and get you back on this earth.*

I'm so very glad I dream about you so much. I still love you dearly and deeply. It hurts so much.

3/8/2011

I had another dream (one of many!) that we won the lottery. You had contributed a couple of dollars, and consequently were going to win $2,000 of the pot that our family would receive. You jumped out of the passenger seat of a car in our driveway, and I watched you run up to the house with a huge smile on your face. You were about eight or nine years old.

So nice to see you in my dreams so often.

I love you so.

I've always been one to remember my dreams and to dream quite vividly. But these dreams I was constantly having of you were so very realistic, I almost felt as if I'd been transported to another plane and had some nocturnal experience that was quite real.

I was also quite convinced that I could somehow get you back. I knew rationally and logically that it was not physically possible, yet there was this determination and strong belief that also co-existed within me that I could in fact find a way.

Shortly after the lottery dream, I purchased a lottery ticket (which was very much outside my norm since as a rational person, I know that my chances of getting struck by lightning are far more probable than winning the lottery). Since this was quite rare for me, I didn't quite know how to read the Mega Millions ticket (I know that sounds dumb for a college-educated person), and I remember that feeling of complete surprise when my numbers matched! At the time, this discovery delighted me mainly because of the dream and not because of the money. It was confirming my thoughts that in fact, time, physics, and logic could bend if I put enough spiritual vibration into it.

Ultimately, though, I re-checked my ticket against the online breakdown of that date's winning numbers and concluded I was looking at the wrong date. Not discouraged in the least, I threw the ticket away. Now all these years later, I wonder if I made a mistake on the date and had in fact won, not millions, but thousands, just as the dream predicted. That dream was so visceral, and I was so convinced that so much was possible. It felt good to vibrate at that frequency and have such vivid connections with Aaron. To this very day, I still dream of him often and I've been told by a spiritual medium that he visits me every night standing in the bedroom doorway. I like that idea very much.

3/21/2011

This past weekend was tough.
This was not how I envisioned your 21ˢᵗ birthday to pan out at all.

Your friends had a party in your honor on Saturday night and came to the cemetery on Sunday. They said they're sending me a card and some photos. They also said that they waited until midnight on Saturday night and then stood in a circle when it became your birthday and went around the room and each told a story about you.

Dan and I watched the moon rise on Saturday night out at camp at Uwharrie and I learned today that the moon was the largest it's been in 18 years. The clouds were very dramatic and gray and were all backlit by the moon. As I lay there in my chaise watching the sky, I thought to get up and put on "Till I Can Gain Control Again," when all of a sudden before I could stand up, out of some 2000 songs on the iPod, it came on! As I laid there in wonder and awe, I saw the letters, MOM in the clouds! As the song ended, they began to diffuse, and the moment was gone.

You are always in my heart and my thoughts, and I know how your spirit is always nearby.

I love you now and forever, and your name will be on my lips when I take my last breath.

Mom

This is my crude drawing from my journal. Dan saw the cloud word too, and I'm glad I took the time to quickly sketch it out because I don't think I'd believe it really happened now. That's me in the chaise on the left and Dan in the chair on the right by the fire.

3/25/2011

I think you got mad at me last night. I went to Donna and Charlie's for dinner and said some unkind sort of things about your dad (for which I was immediately ashamed), and also made a comment that made me look good while making him look less so. It bothered me, and when I got home,

I laid in bed alone (Dan was at horse camp), and about 10:45, suddenly, the smoke alarm went off with a piercing shrill. My heart was pounding like crazy—it scared me so badly! My immediate thought was you and that you were aggravated with me. The noise abruptly stopped and I laid there, heart thudding, wondering what to do.

About ten minutes later, it went off again, but only again for about one minute. I climbed up on our bureau to try to reach the smoke alarm and shut it off, but the cover refused to budge, so I called Dan. By now it was almost midnight, and I was fairly sure he'd never hear the phone ring (which he didn't). As I was leaving him a message, it went off again!

So, I packed up my pillow and earplugs and went upstairs to the guest room. I laid there telling you how sorry I was, and I asked my guardian angels to prevent the alarm from going off again. I never heard it again the rest of the night or the next day.

Sorry! I deserved that!

That was a strange incident and one that I still remember quite vividly. Dan had left a few days ahead of me for horse camp where I was to meet him on Friday afternoon. Dan's mom and dad were kind to invite me over for dinner while he was away, but during some after dinner conversation I mouthed off about Rick, my ex, which instantly made me feel very uncharitable and small. I had been annoyed for a long time that Rick managed to fill Aaron's head with some false stories about our breakup, and that Aaron had held these untruths against me for many years. Yet it was water under the bridge now, and it made me feel like I was somehow hurting Aaron's feelings by bringing it up to my in-laws.

Alone in our big house that night without so much as the dog to keep me company, I drifted off to sleep quickly. When the smoke alarm went off, I sat up like a shot. It was unimaginably loud, and at one point, a mechanical voice repeatedly announced, "FIRE, FIRE, FIRE!" I have no idea why it suddenly stopped, but I remember worrying that it wasn't going to be the last of it. And indeed, it wasn't. Shortly after the first raucous episode, another started in. This happened several times and I was out of options except for talking to Aaron about it. I apologized for being ugly about his dad and asked him to do whatever he could do to make the fire alarm stop going off because it was scaring me. After talking to him, I remember a sense of peace and calm washing over me, and I somehow knew that the fire alarm was going to remain quiet.

And quiet it remained. That fire alarm had never gone off prior to that night, never went off after that night, and upon inspection, Dan later could find nothing wrong with it that would have made it go off for no reason. He also knew nothing of a mechanical voice feature that would shout, "FIRE" either! A woman I later talked to who was able to connect with Aaron psychically told me that he was teasing me. It would be just like him to scare me but then let up when he realized I truly was rattled. From that point on I always made sure to tell him how I liked him to communicate with me!

4/4/2011

This poem was posted on your Facebook page:

About ten days ago

After we saw you

You came back in a dream.

I'm all right now you said…

And it was you, although

You were fleshed out again.

You hugged us all round then,

And gave your welcoming beam.

How like you to be kind.

Seeking to reassure.

And yes, how like my mind

To make itself secure.

~Thom Gunn ("Reassurance," *The Man With Night Sweats*)

I really liked that poem. All except for the last line. It hit home too closely because I was living in a world where Aaron was connecting with me in creative and unimaginable ways, but I kept returning to that place of doubt and insecurity. To that place where I'd been taught a bunch of black and white 'truths,' and not to a place of possibilities that remain to be discovered. Metaphysics, science, and quantum physics were and are continuing to point to new unseen truths, but at the time all these ideas were at war with what I'd been taught to believe about the finality of life and the impossibility of miracles for all but Jesus.

4/14/2011

I opened a book today, and this verse was on the dedication page. It brought tears to my eyes:

"There is hope for your future," says the Lord, "and your children shall come back to their own country."
~Jeremiah 31:17 (Revised Standard Version)

How I wish you would and could come back again in the flesh.

I love you, honey. Please keep nudging me, visiting me, and coming to me in my dreams. Thank you for watching over me.

5/30/2011 - Memorial Day

Aaron's fatal accident occurred on Memorial Day, but in 2010, it was on 5/31. As I rounded the bend to face the first anniversary of his passing, I realized I had the unenvious reality of facing two death dates nearly every year: 5/31 and the actual date of Memorial Day in any given year.

On Memorial Day of 2011, I was still quite raw from it all. My upstairs office was my safe haven for tears and memories of him. No one was on hand to console me, and I could soak my desk with private tears. I did this nearly every day, and crying it out always left me feeling lighter, fresher, and just a tiny bit stronger.

Dan and I had decided to mark the first anniversary of Aaron's passing by hosting a balloon release at our home.[1] We expected about 30 of his and our friends to attend. Dan said he was going to pick up the balloons we'd ordered and asked if I felt like I'd be alright while he was gone. I'm sure he realized the state I was in even though I worked hard to maintain a stiff upper lip while in the company of others. I remember feeling glad that I could have a little bit of alone-time to get some of my tears out and I headed up to my office where I thought my thoughts and wept in solitude. I penned this in my journal:

Please come back, please find a way.

This hurts too much. Life is so different.

WHY???

I recall specifically communicating with Aaron and asking him to find a way to let me know he was near to me today.

63

After my tears and time spent communicating with Aaron, I realized Dan would be on his way back. I picked myself up and decided I should test the song we intended to play when everyone would simultaneously let go of their balloons in a few hours. And behold, a truly incredible thing happened. Here is how it's described in my journal:

Shortly after I wrote the words above, I went downstairs and queued up the song I wanted to play at the balloon release, "I Know You're Out There Somewhere," by the Moody Blues.

I remember grabbing the iPod and thumbing through to the Moody Blues song and placing the iPod with the queued-up song on the speaker dock on a table on our screened porch near where we were planning to release the balloons. I could see "I Know You're Out There Somewhere" on the iPod's display screen and I adjusted the volume to a level I thought would be right. I then took the iPod's remote and walked out of the screened porch to the approximate spot in the yard where I would be standing during the release and hit the button to play the song. To my utter astonishment, something else happened. Here's how I recorded it in my journal:

*Yet when I hit play, out of literally thousands of songs on our iPod, **"Near To You"** by Susan Ashton came on instead.*

Thank you for listening to me, for being here, and for nudging me when I needed it most.

I hope you'll take some time to look up the words to "Near To You." It's a beautiful song that talks about choices. And it was so incredibly beautiful that it played at that very time, that very day, and after my very specific request to Aaron.

Aaron had let me know he was near to me on that first anniversary. I was thunderstruck. But it was instances like this that added up and made me begin to realize he was indeed still in existence. Not in the flesh where I could touch him and hold him, but as near to me as a breeze blowing across my face. Too many things that shouldn't and couldn't happen (according to our conventional thinking) were in fact happening. And they were happening to me!

The seeds of hope were beginning to germinate in the darkness.

There is a quote by Billy Graham featured in the dc Talk TobyMac song, *In My Mind's Eye*, that resonates so deeply. If you have a minute, look up the lyrics to the entire song; it's well worth it. Here's the snippet that contains the Billy Graham quote:

> Can you see God?
> You haven't seen Him?
> I've never seen the wind.
> I see the effects of the wind,
> But I've never seen the wind.
> There's a mystery to it.
> ~Billy Graham

6/16/2011

Last week while driving in the car I was listening to the oldies station where every song is familiar. However, just as I was thinking about Aaron and how he often speaks to me through music, a song I'd never heard came on. The title was, "Mama, I'm Coming Home," by Ozzy Osbourne.

Ok, hurry up please.

Jack is due to be born in a few days—is there a connection?

I was pretty stunned that "Mama, I'm Coming Home" came on just as I was thinking so strongly of Aaron. This was still a time in my journey where I believed I could and would somehow get him back in the flesh and blood. It was so surreal to hear the words to that song. But I felt comforted and believed that somehow Aaron was sending messages to me. Nudging me to gently know everything was OK.

The reference to Jack is to Aaron's step-brother who was born approximately 10 months after Aaron's accident. He's the son of my ex-husband and a woman who was a friend of Aaron's. I can just hear what Aaron would have to say about all that business!

6/30/2011

Yesterday I was sitting on the front porch enjoying the two gardens when I remembered that I had planned to dedicate one of them to Aaron. As I pondered over which one would be the right one, a huge dragonfly made the choice. He landed in the bed with the Japanese Maple, Aaron's lilies, and the dragonfly stepping stone.

I think I will get a small statue of something to add to the garden.

The reason I was reminded of this was that when I went outside, I brought the dogs with me, and Sam immediately stepped down from the porch and laid down in the garden "with the sun on her coat" just like Aaron said.

It's winter inside,
And I don't know if
Spring will ever come.
But every once in a while
I think I see a sprig of green
Pushing up through the frozen ground.
Maybe, just maybe

Spring will come.
Be with me, God,
While I watch for Spring.
Be with me, God,
When the icy winds blow.
Be with me God
When I slip and fall.
Help me to endure the winter.
Help me to wait for Spring.
Help me to give hope a chance.
Help me to live again.
~Author Unknown

8/1/2011

It was weird taking our long-talked-of vacation to the Bahamas without you physically with us. The kids act as if life is absolutely normal and like they never give you so much as a backward glance. I doubt that's really true, but that is the way it seems. Meanwhile, I feel a constant weight on my heart. One day while snorkeling, I cried and got my mask all full of snot and tears just thinking of how much I missed you being there. You would've loved seeing the shark I saw and all the other pretty fish.

Last week after we got back, I was reading my __Hello From Heaven__ book which discusses after death communication, and I was talking to you in my mind saying how much I wished you'd nudge me more when all of sudden the lights went up really bright in the room and the exercise bike went completely haywire and the display started flashing all kinds of crazy things on it and wouldn't work. I had just replaced the batteries about two-three months ago, and normally I only have to replace them every 12-18 months!

But I always want more. More validation, and also to see you in my dreams or to experience a visitation.

Your younger brother, Jack, was born on Dan's birthday. How I pray that he'll have a decent life. I hope I get to meet him one day soon.

Last night Dan and I re-watched the movie, <u>The Secret</u>. There was a scene where there was a picture of a note and it said, "Mama, this will help you. Xoxo."

How I wish that you would give Dan guidance on what to do for a business. This time for some reason, I feel like he needs to find his path without me giving too much guidance or getting involved. It was helpful to him to watch the video too, but I'm asking you and my spirit guides to impress strongly on his mind what to do and which way to go and that he'll be an overwhelming success. That would be so nice.

Gratitude Journal for today:

That you were my son.

And so many other things...Dan, his parents, and kids, our animals, beautiful house and grounds, our good health, that we can laugh together, and so much more!

The aftermath of the financial crisis of 2008 was still in full swing, and we had decided that Dan shouldn't continue to build small subdivisions as the housing sector had been severely affected. Fortunately, we hadn't been affected with what was then our current subdivision—all our contracts held in place to completion of the building process—but we knew it was time for him to do something different. And so, we began thinking about building a cemetery. We knew we still wanted to be involved in some form of land development, and oddly enough, the thought of helping others through the death of a loved one felt very compelling and compassionate to us.

We ultimately purchased an existing 30-acre cemetery just minutes from our house. That was 2012. We've since built a funeral home in the center of the property and are now helping families and individuals on an even more significant scale.

Some folks run from their grief; others lean into it. I think we just had to explore it, experience it, and ultimately find a way to help others through what we felt was one of the most difficult things people face.

8/11/2011

I finally had a dream about you last night. It's been a long dry spell without seeing you in a dream episode—at least ones that I could remember when I woke up. I'm glad this one occurred toward morning so I could remember it and relish it. (Perhaps I've been dreaming of you all along, but only remembered this one.)

Anyway, you were younger in this dream—maybe 15ish, and you lived with your dad in New York City. I came to your apartment one morning to visit you before school. You were excited because you'd ordered a gelato for breakfast (someone was going to deliver it), and also because your new school schedule didn't have you starting in the mornings until 10 a.m. I encouraged you to use the extra time in the morning for studying (knowing all the while I said it that it was most certainly not what you would do).

The very best part of the dream, though, was that I could touch you. We were hugging and I could smell your soft scent.

My heart aches with missing you. Thank you for listening to my pleas for some touch from you. I'm so glad for this dream.

I love you always,
Mom

8/17/2011

Sadness is due to loss more than fear. We can only lose what we thought we owned—physically, emotionally—there are lots of ways of owning.

Go to the heart center and solidify the contact through love to help mitigate the sense of loss. The only thing missing is the body—the contact and connection is maintained throughout lifetimes.

I know that I will "see" Aaron again, but in the meantime my love for him has never ended. The heart never leaves.

I was reading a lot and I think some of the ideas I expressed in my journal came from the research and reading that I was doing on death, grief, and life after death. It was clearly giving me a lot to consider and digest, and although my emotions were primarily charged with grief, I was clearly developing some thoughts around the philosophy of life and the afterlife.

8/22/2011

I met your baby brother, Jack, yesterday. I really thought he was great. In fact, he's the first baby since you that I've actually thought was cute and was drawn to.

I wish you were here to meet him, but of course, I think you already know him and you're watching over him.

I love you honey,
Mom

8/26/2011

I'm getting what I think are two signals—1. I keep seeing and hearing mourning doves all over the place, and 2. I keep getting nudged to meditate.

I looked up the symbolism of the mourning dove and found a connection with mothers, and that the times they coo—morning and evening—are when the veils between the two worlds are the thinnest! The dove symbolizes peace and hope of a new beginning. I'm to listen to their call within my soul in order to discern my personal message.

I wonder if the dove is my power animal, and I wonder if you are trying to connect with me—your hard of hearing, nearsighted, and too earthbound mom.

I love you—keep talking to me and watching over me.

I found the following online regarding mourning doves as totems:

- Bringer of peace and love, understanding of gentleness, spirit messenger, communication between the two worlds, maternity.
- The dove represents peace of the deepest kind. It soothes and quiets our worried and troubled thoughts, and enables us to find renewal in the silence of the mind.
- The dove's singing is its most distinctive characteristic, to be heard throughout the day, as well as first thing in the morning and last thing at night. According to mystical and magical traditions, the veils between the physical and spiritual worlds are then at their thinnest. Their coo sounds mournful, possibly reflecting hidden emotions within those with this medicine. How you perceive its sound often mirrors the energies that are present in your life.
- Dove teaches us that regardless of external circumstances, peace is always a touch away— within us, and always available.

- The dove embodies maternal instinct and is connected to Mother Earth and her creative energies. Their mournful coo speaks to our deepest self and stirs our emotions. The voice of the dove is a rain song bringing us hope of a new beginning. Listen for their call with your soul.
- If a dove flies into your life, you are being asked to go within and release your emotional disharmony, be it of the past or the present. Dove helps us to rid trauma stored within our cellular memory.
- Doves carry the energy of promise. When inner agitation is banished from our thoughts, words, and feelings, goodness awaits us. So we are able to receive the gifts doves present us, healing on all levels—emotionally, physically, mentally, spiritually. It is of utmost importance.

~Ina Woolcott (*Shamanic Journey.com*)

8/30/2011

I had a really nice dream about you last night. Once again, you were younger—maybe nine—and I can remember hugging you, smelling your hair and skin, and telling you how very much I loved you. There was an almost overwhelming sense of deep, deep love between us, and it made me feel so good.

Despite all the good things and the things I know about life after death, this is still really, really hard and my heart still feels heavy.

I keep putting one foot in front of the other, though, and looking to learn and grow and endure.

9/28/2011

I woke up this morning to the alarm right in the middle of a dream of you. You were young again, lying on your stomach and I was touching

your head. I could see your long, bare back and it felt so good to be near
you and to touch you again.
I really didn't want to wake up.

On Monday I came into my office along with Sam when we both
suddenly heard a very loud thump. Dan called to me from his office asking
me what the noise was. At first, I couldn't figure it out, then I noticed Sam
looking very warily at my office doorway. She then cowered low and ran
out of my office. I knew if it were you, she wouldn't have been afraid,
and the thump was actually the wood floor creaking with what sounded
like a lot of weight. All I can figure is Ron Bartol. I'd been talking with
Joyce on Sunday, and she had said lots of people have had an after-death
contact from him, so that night I asked him to come to me. And I think
he did.
Your weight would have never made the floor pop like that.

I miss you so much my boy.

Ron Bartol was the father of one of my very best friends. I
basically grew up spending the vast majority of my time at he
and his wife, Joyce's, house which was situated on our local
lake just a couple blocks from where I lived with my mom and
dad. In the summer we water skied and swam, and in the
winter we ice-skated and snowmobiled. Ron and Joyce were as
dear to me as my BFF, Suzi. They never over-parented, but
always kept us safe and ensured we were having a LOT of
fun. I was devastated in 2003 to receive the phone call alerting
me to his death in a motor vehicle accident. I always felt like
Ron and Joyce loved me like a daughter, and I remember
silently reaching out to him across the ether asking him to pay
me a visit. When that floor popped and Aaron's dog's hackles
raised and she stared in that doorway, it immediately struck
me that I was being graced with that requested visit.

2/16/2012

We are not human beings having a spiritual experience;
We are spiritual beings having a human experience.
~Pierre Teilhard deChandon

There is a land of the living and a land of the dead and the
bridge is love,
the only survival, the only meaning.
~Thornton Wilder

2/28/2012

I was seeking help from every quarter. I consumed books, I researched, and I also sought out a few spiritual mediums hoping they would provide some evidentiary words that would help me connect with Aaron. I had a reading on 2/28/2012 in which the medium said Aaron fiddles with the candles around my house and makes the flames do funny things including blowing them out. Here's what I recorded in my journal a couple of days later:

After this meeting, I lit a candle. It immediately went up into a high flame and started throwing out black smoke. The smoke alarms then started going off all over the house!

That same night after dinner, I went into the dining room, flipped on the light, and noticed that one of the three chandelier lights was out. As I reached up to unscrew the bulb, I had a strong feeling there was actually nothing wrong with it at all. I twisted it, and of course, it lit right back up!

Then the next morning, I shut the upstairs hall light off, walked downstairs, but for some reason glanced back upstairs only to find that the light was back on. Wow!

It's easy to discount these types of happenings as mere coincidences, or figments of our imaginations or troubled minds, however, I've found that I've had too many 'coincidences' and 'figments' for them to be random chance. There's so much more to life than we know—even in the 21st century (just read a little about quantum physics if you need to convince yourself)—and I think we can do ourselves a lot of good by being open to the signs and wonders—the little miracles—that happen all around us all the time.

3/2/2012

Cruelty is fear in disguise and nothing more.
Fear is nothing more than failure of the imagination.
~Timothy Findley (*Not Wanted on the Voyage*)

7/1/2012

As I sit in heaven, and watch you every day, I try and let you
know with signs,

I never went away. I hear you when you're laughing, and I
watch you as you sleep;

I even place my arms around you to calm you as you weep.

I see you wish the days away begging to have me home. So I
try to send you signs so you know you're not alone. Don't feel
guilty that you have life that was denied to me.

Heaven is truly beautiful, just you wait and see!

So live your life, laugh again, enjoy yourself, be free.

Then I know with every breath you take, you'll be taking one
for me.
~Hazel Birdsall

7/11/2012

We chase wild dreams and long for all that eludes us, when the
greatest joys are within our grasp, if we can only recognize
them.
~Ben Sherwood

We all shine on in the moon and the stars and the sun.
~John Lennon

Trust your heart if the seas catch fire and live by love though
the stars walk backward.
~e.e. cummings

Once they walked among us, laughing, yelling, keeping watch.
We knew them. We spoke to them. We took them by the hand.
We loved them. They were our friends, our families, our
heroes. Now in the crumbled earth, they are our memories,
remaining in this world if not visible to it. They wait for us
along their shaded avenues; secluded as only urban dwellers
can know seclusion among the many, within the perplexing
grids laid out by those in whose care the remembrance of
their history—of their existence—we have entrusted our dead.

As we walk among the temples, towers, and stone blocks
which are their witness in this time after their time, a rushing
wind may stir their voices.

The voices come not from the grave, but from within our own,
quick, flesh-encased bones. The murmurs we hear are the
murmurs of those we have lost made part of us.
~William Gilmore Simms

10/11/2012

It's a good day today—10/11/12—and so it's auspicious that I saw you last night. I really feel like it was more of a visitation than a dream because I was fully aware that you had passed away and that it was incredible that I was seeing you.

I was in a kitchen, and you were in an adjoining room and were a young boy playing with Preston. You looked directly into my eyes and said, "Hi, Mom" and "I love you." I told you I loved you, and in the dream went running to Dan to tell him I'd seen you!

You had that one red shirt on you always used to wear.

I've had a lot of instances this week where I've felt your presence.

We're going to see a medium, Theresa Caputo, two weeks from today, and I hope to feel you there with us as well.

I do love you and miss you every day.

12/12/2012

Somewhere, somewhere in time's own space, there must be some sweet pastured place. Where creeks sing on and tall trees grow, some paradise where horses go. For by the love that guides my pen, I know great horses live again.
~Stanley Harrison

God love Prana; bless him and keep him in your care until we meet again.

We had lost our dear, sweet colt, Prana, to a freak accident in the pasture. It was heartbreaking to see him struggling for breath and shivering in the night air despite the blanket we put on him. The doctors were kind and tried hard to help, but when we said we thought it would be the most merciful thing we could do to put him down, all of them slid their hands down his flanks and with heads held low, quietly said they agreed. He trusted us as we led him to that softly padded space where we sent him from this world to the next. We drove home in silence in the middle of the night and cried buckets of tears for our sweet palomino colt. It seemed so unfair to endure the loss of another dear family member.

12/27/2012

Tough Christmas season this year.
Missing you and feeling angry and exhausted a lot of the time.

We had another reading with Beth B. today, but not much evidence there at all, and felt very scattered—just like my mind.

I do feel like I'm supposed to quit looking for you though. I need to accept

what has happened, and quit trying to prove to myself over and over that
you still live.
I need to just leave it be.

I just feel sad and empty, and I want to feel happy and peaceful. I think
it's up to me to change, but I want a miracle.

1/7/2013

From The Eagle and the Rose. Grey Eagle, spirit guide, says these things:

...Purpose of our lives here on earth is to learn and grow.
...Look within [to determine how].

Your world needs gentleness. ...The universe shakes and
becomes brighter [as we do this].

Be still... be quiet... and listen... to your soul... [for it]
whispers to you [in stillness]. Accept the responsibility of your
soul and your own spiritual growth, for you and no
other...have the power to be still.

Turn your face to the light [God], for in that light you will find
warmth. ...You will find healing.

...And you will find love.

Accept that all things given are a gift for you and part of your
learning process.

Take your courage in your hands and step into the light. Turn
your face to the sun and allow God's light to shine down upon
you. For you are children of God, and as children, if you
reach out your hand, God will take it, and He will hold it firm
and He will steer you to a greater understanding of your own
self. And He will give you His strength.

He will not stem the flow of tears, nor will He wash away your pain,

but He will take you to His breast and comfort you.

Come, sit by my fire. Hold out your hands to the flame and be comforted by the warmth of it. But understand that there are many who keep this fire going. My fire needs kindling. My fire needs those of you who will labor. Who will go out and collect kindling to place on the fire?

The fire is there for all, and there are many who will come and sit by the fire. They will warm themselves, they will feel comforted, and then they will turn away to continue their lives.

There are those of you who will come and sit by my fire, and you will marvel at the height of the flames and be grateful for the warmth that the fire gives out.

And when you are truly comforted, you will turn away and continue with your lives.

And then there are those of you who will come and sit by my fire, and you will see how tall the flames grow. And you gain comfort from the warmth of the flames. And when you have been comforted enough, there are those of you who will then recognize that if the fire is to continue burning, in order that the many should be comforted, then there is work to be done and kindling to be found.

Come all of you, and sit by my fire. We demand nothing from you.

We ask that you give nothing, except only if you want to do so.

Come, sit by my fire and listen to the wise words.

Listen to the crackle of the sticks as the heat of the flame
burns through them.

Watch the sparks fly. Each spark is a light. Each spark is truth.
Each spark is a knowing.

Come, sit by my fire, and I will warm you.

~Rosemary Altea (*The Eagle and the Rose*. Reprinted with
permission.)

I didn't know when I recorded that passage in my journal that
seven years later, in 2020, I would leave a 40+ year career in
financial services and go to work in our newly-built funeral
home. I had no idea then what a privilege it is to help people
through some of the most difficult times and circumstances of
their lives. My mental image of helping those in need always
went to Charon, the boatman, holding up a lamp as he ferried
his passengers across the river, Styx. As I re-read Grey Eagle's
passages, I was drawn to the line about those who sit by the
fire and choose to help keep it burning. I like to think that's
what Dan and I do.

1/11/2013

You are starting to build and populate your eternity on the
other side. Try hard to respect and celebrate that. Focus on
what will be waiting. Not what you feel like you have lost in
the present.
~Scott Miller, friend, upon hearing of the death of Prana

Sometimes we just have to hear what we already know.

4/11/2013

*It's weird how I don't write in here for months at a time now. I think it's
all part of learning how to live with a broken heart. Sometimes I even
come in my office in the morning and fail to greet you right away. I don't
like that. It makes me feel guilty and like I don't love you or you don't
matter anymore which is not the case.*
I found this quote today:

I am open to where the waterway takes me, knowing that
change,
whether good or bad, is part of the journey.
~Author Unknown

5/30/2013

*Memorial Day was this past Monday, and I'm hating the thought that
tomorrow it will be three years. How can that be? You still seem so alive
to me—like you should just walk into my room at any minute and
interrupt me while I'm on the phone. Remember how you used to say,
"Mom, Mom, Mom, Mom, Mom, Mom" repeatedly when you wanted
my attention when I was on the phone? Still makes me smile just like it
did back then.*
*Even though I acted like you were annoying me,
I secretly liked it whenever you wanted me for any reason.* 😊

*I visited the tree last Friday night. To my surprise (maybe not), it was
thriving and was standing there all green, leafy, and tall. The base was
very overgrown and I could just make out one edge of the cross that
Megan made to commemorate you. A cop drove up only seconds later and
asked if I was alright. He was very kind, and in a way, I felt was a gift
from you. He told me to stay strong. Who said I was strong?*

*I've been feeling like I'm hearing from you a lot leading up to Memorial
Day and May 31—which I've certainly been asking for. Oddly, I'm
getting a list of messages about you coming home. You're talking to me*

through music again, and beginning last week, I once again heard the Ozzie Osbourne, "Mama, I'm Coming Home" song—twice in fact, then we went to a movie on Memorial Day where we saw previews for a movie called "Now You See Me," and right under those words is the date May 31! Then yesterday again I got in the car, and not once but twice, I heard other songs I've never heard before about 'coming home.' That plus Kellie called me to say she saw you while she meditated on Friday night.

So, what does it all mean? Well, if you are coming home, I just hope I recognize you. Maybe you'll have that little freckle right in the middle of your nose—or those big sweet brown eyes. Or maybe you'll still be able to "do voices" and make me laugh.

I do still love you and miss you so.

Thank you for your other-worldly help and protection though.

Love Always, Mom

She was no longer wrestling with the grief, but could sit down
with it as a lasting companion
and make it a sharer in her thoughts.
~George Eliot

Sometimes I actually feel like this.

5/31/2013

How can it be three years since I've last seen you? It doesn't seem possible, and of course it doesn't seem right. My heart aches for you, but at the same time, I don't want to live a sad, depressed, ungrateful life because I don't think that would honor you at all.

In a book I recently read called <u>Wild</u>, the author, Cheryl Strayed, recounts how she had lost her mom at an early age. She decided to hike the Pacific Coast Trail—a grueling walk from the Mexican border to Oregon. She did it alone and faced many perils including rattlesnakes, bears, and predatory hunters. When she entered the Mount Hood wilderness in Oregon, she wrote this:

"I went to the river and squatted down and splashed my face. It was narrow and shallow here, so late in the summer and so high up, barely bigger than a stream. Where was my mother, I wondered. I'd carried her so long, staggering beneath her weight. On the other side of the river, I let myself think. And something inside of me released."

I know Aaron's on the other side of the river, but will I ever experience that release? Where it's ok that he's there and I'm here and all the things I'd hoped and dreamed for his life—and mine—lie crushed at the base of a tree on the morning of
Monday May 31, 2010?

I don't want my heart to hold heavy with grief. I want to hold what once was lightly in an open palm and feel secure that what I believe will indeed be.

10/11/2013

He was sure that the paths were not too difficult or strenuous for you. This is the blessed life—not anxious to see far down the road or overly concerned about the next step, not eager to choose the path nor weighted down with the heavy responsibilities of the future, but quietly following the shepherd, one step at a time.
~C.E. Cowman (*Streams In the Desert*)

For peace, walk in nature.
For truth, ask a child.
For serenity, be yourself.
~Author Unknown

All we are seeking is our own permission to be who we are.

12/2/2013

Reach out your hand if your cup be empty. If your cup is full,
let it be again. Let it be known there is a fountain that was not
made by the hands of man.
~Robert Hunter ("Ripple" sung by the Grateful Dead)

12/24/2013

*Missing you at Christmas and always. I was glad you appeared in a
dream the other night, even if it was only a short snippet.*

*I was also glad you amazed our staff and friends on 12/14 at Dan's
office dinner party.
Just to recount:*

*When Dan began toasting various people, I noticed the candle in front of
me went out and smoke went up in a vertical column. Not wanting to
interrupt the toast, I did nothing, but I then began to notice that with each
new toast, the column of smoke would seem to reinvigorate and send up a
new column of renewed smoke. I thought it odd that a candle that had
gone out could do such a thing.*

*When we finally got to the end of the toasting, I stood up and mentioned
to the entire table what I'd been seeing. Others commented that they had
noticed too. I said that I couldn't help but think it was Aaron, and as soon
as I said that, the candle burst into flame—as if it had never gone out
at all!*

It happened again when I said, "Look, there he is now!"—again a renewed burst of flame! There were a lot of tears at the table—and chill bumps too, but why wouldn't you be offering these sincere people, our staff and friends, who truly care about those who have crossed over and those whom they've left behind?

Please be with all of us tonight as we celebrate the miracle of Christmas and the togetherness of family. I love you forever, my son.

Mom

2/10/2014

Dad's birthday. Funny, I don't think about him that much, but I think he did turn up in a dream last night. I know mom was in a dream because I remember that vividly. But today, I talked with Brandy P. (from work) who lost her 14-year-old son, Tyler, just before Christmas. At one point in the conversation, I had some very strong impressions from Tyler that he was very sorry for having taken his own life, and that it was a very in-the-moment thing he had done. I was saying to Brandy that these impressions were coming from my heart and not my head when suddenly, two mourning doves landed directly in front of me on the back porch deck, not two feet away. This is particularly incredible because: 1) Doves don't do that. 2) Just this morning, I was reminding myself of how I seem to see/hear mourning doves at the start and end of every day and how thankful I was for their reminder to me of Aaron on the other side. 3) Just before meeting with Brandy, I decided to meditate just a little bit and asked Aaron as well as Tyler to come through if they wanted and to guide the conversation and help me to be of help to Brandy.

When I was telling Brandy my impressions of Tyler's taking of his own life, first one mourning dove (Aaron?) and then another (Tyler?) lighted down on the deck in front of me.

Incidentally a red bird hit the glass door to the bedroom yesterday and then

stayed sitting on the deck floor for a very long time afterward before she
flew away completely unharmed. Who was that?

In addition to dragonflies as I mentioned earlier, mourning doves began showing up in my life after Aaron passed. When I once again researched the symbolism of the mourning dove, I found some more interesting things—slightly different nuances from what I'd found previously:

- The dove is believed by nearly all cultures to be associated with feminine energy, particularly maternal energy.
- Native Americans used to watch for doves, particularly at dusk because they would visit water sources at that time of day. Water is also believed to possess maternal energy.
- The 'between times' of the day—dawn and dusk— are when we often hear the dove cooing. It is at dawn and dusk that the veil between the physical and spiritual world is the thinnest. Spending time in meditation and communing with our loved ones who've crossed over during these sacred times of day may bring us much peace and comfort. And we may even receive a message—a thought, idea, or inspiration, or perhaps even a physical sign.
  ~NativeAmericanTotems.com

5/18/2014

One of my classmates lost her husband the other day, andI read the
following on his blog post:

"The bitterest tears that are shed on graves are for deeds left undone and
words left unsaid."

It's really easy to get caught up in the immediacy of life, and I think it's impossible to constantly live in a state of awareness and deliberate kindness for those we love, but I do think it's possible to begin an awareness practice. Just for five minutes a day. Begin by setting aside five minutes for alone time. Use the time to set your intentions for the day, send up thoughts and prayers for those whom you love, and just be very present. Feel your breath, hear the quiet sounds around you, and feel the surface you're sitting, lying, or standing on. You'll emerge from this small act much calmer and more prepared for the day. And you will likely even remember to say and do some kind things to and for the ones you love. Remember that a journey of a thousand miles starts with just one step!

8/18/2014

Just returned home from Wisconsin where we laid my brother, Michael, to rest after a tough battle with Alzheimer's disease. The memorial for Michael was both beautiful and fitting and I was honored to have been able to help out.

I've had several nudges from Michael already, including feathers literally falling from the sky virtually into our laps; signs reading "heaven" right in front of us; a visitation in which I saw a younger (30-something) Michael looking right into my eyes; lights going out three times in a row (each time with me being able to snap the switch back into the on position when neither I nor anyone else had switched it off); and this morning back at home pulling up the Facebook posting of the Chinese lantern we sent up for him last week in Wisconsin when my computer suddenly began making a very loud noise that was impossible to shut off. (Eventually I had to shut the entire computer down to get it to stop.)

I am glad I'm on the watch for these signs and only wish Beverly (Michael's wife and my sister-in-law) could allow herself to open up to the possibilities of communication from Michael from the Great Beyond.

It was clear to me on that visit to Wisconsin that she remains very much in love with him.

Please keep in touch with me brother.

Some time later, I asked Beverly if she was still watching for Michael and if she felt like she'd heard from him at all. She astonished me by saying that nearly every night she awakens to the weight of someone sitting down on the edge of the bed. He stays for a little while and then goes away again. This went on for many months and I felt like it gave her great comfort.

I've always loved this picture of my brother on horseback while hunting elk in Montana. I was probably only 12 or 13 years old when he made the trip, and I can remember being green with envy that he was riding horses and living in the wilderness for days on end (not so much the hunting of elk)!

12/29/2014 - Eleven-Five

On 11/5/2014 we lost my beloved mother-in-law, Donna. She and I had had a long-standing agreement that after she passed, she would make sure to let me know that she was still alive and well on the other side.

A couple of weeks went by, and although I'd expected some immediate contacts from her, I'd heard nothing. I began reminding her of our agreement and urging her to please get in touch. Well, sure enough about three weeks after her death, lights all over the house started going haywire. I'd turn them on and they'd promptly go off all by themselves. Brand new strands of Christmas lights would work one minute and then inexplicably go off the next, only to come back on the next day. I even had one light bulb snap at the neck (all on its own) and remain wedged in the socket and had to replace an entire receptacle. She also made her feelings very clear on the distribution of her jewelry. Karen and Kellie, my sisters-in-law (and Donna's daughters) took the "good jewelry" and divided it amongst themselves as well as gave a piece each to Katelyn and Megan (Donna's granddaughters). They then very generously decided to let the rest of us girls (i.e., Donna's daughters-in-law) in the family take turns at picking out pieces of the remaining jewelry and dividing it amongst ourselves. While doing our round-robin picking, it occurred to me to perhaps pick out one thing for Dan's ex-wife, Donna's ex-daughter-in-law. However, I heard a very strong NO! in my mind and immediately dismissed the idea. Later, when Megan (my stepdaughter and Donna's granddaughter) arrived and I gave her the jewelry I'd picked out for her, she said, "Maybe I'll give a piece to my mom," and no sooner was that utterance out of her mouth when the lights on the front half of the house immediately went out. The entire Christmas tree went dark, the light in the closet that I'd flipped on went off, and Dan said, "Wow, I guess Grandma doesn't think that's a very good idea!"

Wow, is right! I put a lot of stock in Dan's reaction as well—his immediate thought was that she was saying no for a second time and for whatever reason!

Grandpa (my father-in-law) has also been listening to his thoughts. About a week or so after Donna's death, he was working in his office when he suddenly got a very strong thought to go wind up the cuckoo clock and get it running again after almost a month of not being wound. When he went to wind it and get it started up, he noted that the clock read 11:05—the date of her death! She also communicated that date to him again recently when he was lying in bed and of all things, the floaters in his eyes formed a pattern:

11514 Sullivan

I love that she is connecting, and I wish that Aaron would give me a nudge as I haven't had one from him in a while.

Love you always Donna!

PS: Last night we had spaghetti dinner in honor of what would have been her 79ᵗʰ birthday! (Donna was very proud of her spaghetti even though she used Ragu and boxed pasta! And we all loved it!)

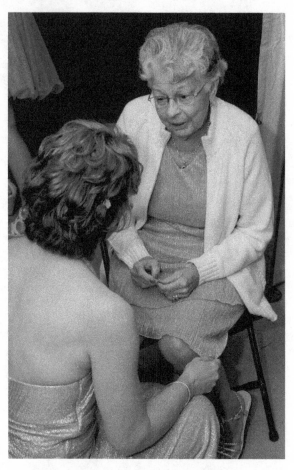

Donna and me at my wedding. She wrote on my wedding platter that night, "To our wonderful son & new daughter-in-law—my best friend." That made me feel really good.

Donna's warm inscription is at the top rim of the plate.

7/20/2015

Well, you are not alone in this world…even if you have outlived everyone. I believe that we are surrounded by a host of unseen friends and loved ones, now passed away, who exert an influence upon our lives, and who never abandon us.
~Elizabeth Gilbert (*The Signature of All Things*)

10/30/2015

Perhaps as we grow older, we tend to simplify our lives and prune them of the nonessentials. It's not entirely a matter of choice. Life strips us of most of our youthful illusions and bright dreams, and death takes away, one by one, those whom we loved and upon whom we depended.

If we are to survive, we must reconcile ourselves to this plundering, we must learn to distinguish between those things which were ornamental and the true necessities, and we must learn too the possibly more difficult lesson of letting go gracefully the superficial and of the treasuring and nurturing the few basic realities which must be our support and comfort for as long as we walk about under the light of the heavens. Perhaps that is why, in that moment on the edge of the heath, something responded to this place.
~Author Unknown

11/25/2015

What you resist persists, and what you look at disappears.
~Neale Donald Walsch (*Conversations With God*)

I feel something magical in the air. Thanksgiving, my 57th birthday, the cold, crisp air in the morning, seeing the deer frisk in the woods at daybreak.

I somehow feel a sense of anticipation, exhilaration, and wonder again.
Today is exciting, tomorrow brings possibilities.

You are right where you're supposed to be and you are near to me always.

Love Always,
Mom

I always tell people that grief is a journey. You never really forget how dreadfully difficult it was to lose your loved one, but you learn to carry the grief. And you begin to let joy and wonder seep back into your life while at the same time still loving, honoring, and missing that special person. After all, that's what he or she would really want for us, isn't it?

12/17/2015

We sent our dear Mew-Mew over the rainbow bridge on 12/6/2015
after she became paralyzed on her back end—we think likely due to
an embolism.

I asked very specifically for a sign that involved an orange cat to let me
know that Mew was safe and was in Aaron's arms. My expectations
were low since I was looking for such a specific, unusual sign. However,
within five-seven minutes of making that request on the way home from
the emergency clinic with Mew in a burial box in the back seat, I was
stunned to see two orange kittens playing on the gravel drive at the produce
farm on Highway 73! I've stopped there many times over the years, and
have driven by it nearly five times every week for the past six years and
have never seen one cat there,
nevermind two orange ones!

Less than five days later, we received a nice sympathy card from the
veterinary clinic, and not surprisingly, it featured an orange cat on the front
cover of the card!

Thank you, Mew and Aaron!

When we try to pick out anything by itself, we find it hitched
to everything else in the universe.
~John Muir

This sweet picture of Mew was taken at our
wedding. She was not an orange cat, but for some
reason orange was the color I desired as a sign that
day.

12/21/2015 - "Stranglehold"

*As I was leaving the house for an appointment the other day, I was
thinking about how much I wished I was more deliberate in my high
school and college days about preparing myself for a good job instead of
just aimlessly getting good grades, but with no plan. I was thinking about
how my social life was what was really important to me, and in
particular about Skip (my first love whom I met in high school, now gone
from our time). I mused over how we used to drive his Cobra to Madison
and then drive round and round the Capitol square with the strains of Ted
Nugent's "Stranglehold" blaring out the windows.*

Not two minutes after that scene went through my head, "Stranglehold" came on the radio!

Now that's a song that the oldies station rarely, if ever, plays (except for maybe at 1 a.m.!). I had the widest smile on my face and tears of joy pricking my eyes as I drove down our country roads with Ted Nugent cranked up and blaring out the windows of the Durango!

Thank you, Skip! I loved hearing from you.

Coincidence? I certainly don't think so. Too many of these things happen, and they happen all the time. There's more to all this than meets the eye, and while scientists may not as yet have discovered some of these unseen truths, it doesn't mean they don't exist.

5/4/2016 - Shirley

Yesterday I wore Mom's jade ring that Shirley J. re-wrapped for me a couple years ago. I also wore Dad's jade ring (which my sister-in-law recently unearthed and sent to me). Well remarkably, I just learned that Shirley, who was diagnosed with cancer some months ago, died yesterday surrounded by family who loved her.

Shirley was a great artist, a lovely, generous, and happy human being, and I was glad to be wearing that ring she once wrapped on the day she crossed over. I felt such a nice connection and reassurance of life in the hereafter.

I hope she gives Aaron a big hug from me.

I think it's a mistake to look askance at coincidences. I hadn't worn that jade ring in many months, but for some reason slipped it on my hand the very day Shirley passed.

Just remember that coincidence is God's way of remaining anonymous!

5/31/2016 - Six Years

It was special. We got up yesterday morning and rode to the top of a high meadow that has some of the best views in all of the Appalachians in my opinion. We sat with the sun coming up, cooked breakfast, and just connected with Aaron.

Then, last night when we got back from horse camp, we took some wine and a blanket and went and sat by his grave over there by the pond. The dogs were with us, and as she does nearly every time we're there, Sam (his dog), went and laid directly over his grave. In fact, if Aaron had been lying there on the grass with us, Sam's body would have been lying over his right shoulder and the two of them would have been nose to nose.

As we were talking about it and talking about Aaron, just then a huge dragonfly came right over us and spent quite a bit of time darting back and forth over where our little party was sitting on the grass. Later, Dan walked to the pond for a minute and I started talking out loud to Aaron asking him to come to me in my dreams because he always used to and I haven't had a dream of him in quite some time now. Well, this morning I woke up saying his name over and over and over because I was having a dream about him and I was calling him to come to me in the dream. Amazing. Amazing grace.

It's said that just before daybreak and also at twilight (when day becomes night), the veil between the two worlds is the thinnest. I believe that if we quiet our minds, especially at daybreak and twilight, we can connect with our loved ones who have crossed over. I often ask Aaron to come to me in my dreams as I'm lying in bed before sleep comes. And indeed, I do experience dreams or dream visitations from him very often. The warmth of those visits carries on in my heart and soul every time it happens.

Our sweet Sam lying atop Aaron's earthly resting spot. We don't ask her to do this; she just lies down right on that spot on her own.

6/29/2016

Opened a book called My Neck of the Woods by my beloved author, Louise Dickinson Rich, today, and on page 252 was delighted by this passage:

"They tell us he is lost, but he isn't lost. Lost to us for a time, perhaps, but not lost to God. Listen! 'If I take the wings of the morning and dwell in the uttermost parts of the sea; even there shall Thy hand lead me, and Thy right hand shall hold me fast.' We are only lost for a small space to those we love."
~Psalm 139: 9-10

2/23/2017

Two weeks ago, I found my beloved Patrick lying dead in the cul de sac. I have felt a crushing weight on my heart and a vice grip on my throat much of the time ever since. Then this past Monday, we put nearly 12-year-old Sassy down as she was suffering from cancer. The only comfort has been a visitation from (or maybe just a dream of) Patrick about three nights after his death. No words were spoken, but he was there with me (or I with him! Maybe I was astral traveling!), and I was absolutely and utterly enveloped by LOVE. The feeling soaked through me and it was so unbelievably wonderful. I would have loved to stay right there in that feeling forever.

After we left the vet's office on Monday (from having Sassy euthanized), we pulled into the driveway and there fluttering in front of our windshield was a butterfly. Then Dan noticed our peach tree had one and only one flower on it (that had not been there earlier in the day when I was working outside). Later, I went into my closet and suddenly a little coin purse fell off the shelf and landed at my feet (without me touching anything!), and as I looked at the coin purse, I saw one and only one symbol engraved on it—a heart!

Thank you for these little touches, Sassy and Patrick. Love you always.

Patrick and Sassy were two of our beloved cats. I believe animals can also nudge us from the other side, and we're once again limiting ourselves if we believe only humans have the superior power to do so.

There's a story that author, Linda Kohanov, shares in her book, *The Tao of Equus*, where after the death of her beloved dog, a whippet, she grieved deeply but was finally inspired to bring another dog home. Quite the opposite of a whippet, the new dog was large and shaggy. However, one day while sitting outside together on the deck, Linda was stunned to notice that the shadow-being cast by the new, large, hairy dog, was sleek, thin, and exactly that of a whippet! She had had feelings that somehow her beloved whippet's soul was embodied in the new dog, and what a powerful affirmation she beheld that day in the streaming sunshine.

2/27/2017 - Panda

A story was shared with me by a friend who recently attended a memorial service for a friend that had passed. Her friend's cat, Panda, was in attendance for the service and of his own volition, laid under her memorial table which held her cremains and various photos.

My friend shared that she felt Panda was channeling his human companion, and that just as she had this thought, the cat suddenly let out a very long and soulful meow.

12/29/2017 - Last Page of the First Journal

As this year comes to an end, you still walk in my dreams on occasion, still always a boy.

I don't have as many supernatural things happen. Have I gotten too caught up with the day-to-day that I can't feel that soft tap from the other side?

But when life slows down, my thoughts always turn to you.

Today these words from "Just Breathe" by Willie Nelson touched my heart:

"Yes, I understand that every life must end. As we sit alone, I know someday we must go. ...Hold me till I die; meet you on the other side."

What else is going to happen that I will need to put in another journal?

*Where did the last seven years go?
I guess it's high time I write this book!*

9/20/2019 - Flyleaf

> To hold a grievance against fate accomplishes nothing; things
> occur without reason or rhyme, and no more can be said.
> Railing against such fortune is to censure wood smoke or
> wind, and to be sorrowed through all the days of your passing.
> In the end, there is nothing left except to shoulder whatever
> you have been handed and go on.

~Robert James Waller (*A Thousand Country Roads*)

I transcribed the above on the flyleaf at the end of my journal. I can't recall, but I imagine I wondered if I were going to continue writing down my experiences and my feelings, or if the fact that I filled one journal signified the end of my writing about my grief journey. Beginnings and endings can always feel so unnerving.

As it turns out, I had more to say. And that was because I continued to experience nudges from Aaron and others. And then I began asking other people who would share their special stories with me if I might include them in my journal. No one ever refused, and I knew someday I would finally sit down and put them in a book. I was getting nudges about doing that as well! My only wish is and has been that others will find comfort and hope from these experiences and thoughts.

We love so deeply which is why we hurt so deeply. But there is no end to love.

---

1. I didn't know at the time how destructive those mylar balloons are to our rivers, streams, pastureland, and the animals inhabiting them. I would never do it again!

Scraps

A lso, at the back of my first journal, I tucked a bunch of stories and quotes that I had collected over the years. Here again, I suppose I didn't know I was going to eventually crack open a new journal and start writing more.

Some were just torn scraps of paper; others I had typed up, folded, and tucked in the journal. They're all from various points and times since Aaron's passing, but all of them were relevant and meaningful. I share them here with you.

Mom

I wrote the following letter in December of 2006 as my mother lay dying from cancer in the nursing home in my small hometown in Wisconsin. I've always been thankful that my mom passed prior to Aaron as it would have killed her right then and there if she had lost one of her grandsons. As it was, I suspect she took him into her own arms when he crossed over just three and a half years later:

12/11/2006

Dear Mom:

I hope this letter finds you peaceful, as pain-free as you can be, and in the good care of the folks at the Manor. I can only imagine how difficult this is for you, but I also think of your amazing faith in God and how you've always weathered your circumstances with strength and grace.

You are in my prayers and my thoughts always, and I only wish I could be at your side. I am so glad that Michael has been such a faithful and true son and brother—I think we are both very lucky to have his love and steadfastness.

I don't know if you can use these slippers, but I thought they'd be nice since they're so easy to slip in and out of. Also, I thought some hand cream might feel good to you too. And finally, there are some chocolates that I hope you can nibble at a little— share them with your visitors too.

In closing, here's something from one of my favorite books, <u>Streams in the Desert</u> by L.B. Cowman:

"The hill was steep, but suddenly a narrow winding path appeared. And then the Master said, 'My child, here thou will safely walk with me alone.'
I trembled, yet my heart's deep trust replied, 'So be it, Lord.'

He took my feeble hand in His, and no friend I saw, save Jesus only. So tenderly He led me on and up, and spoke to me such words of cheer, such secret whispers of His wondrous love, that soon I told Him of all my grief and fear. I found my footsteps quickened, and light shined on my rugged way.

...A little while and we shall meet again. With greetings such as here we cannot know, with happy song and heavenly embraces, and we who gather

in the golden streets shall often be stirred to speak with grateful love of that dark day when Jesus bade us climb that narrow, steep hill leaning on Him alone."

'He brought me forth also into a large place;
He delivered me; because He delighted in me.'
~Psalms 18:19

Try to stay strong and calm by keeping your focus on the Lord—He promises to deliver you to a better place. I love you, Mom, and you too, Michael.

Law of Attraction

This is an excerpt from *The Power* by Rhonda Byrne which I shared with some of my gal pals on October 25, 2011 and subsequently printed and tucked in the back of my journal:

Love is not weak, feeble, or soft. Love is the positive force of life!

Love is the cause of everything positive and good.

Everything you want to be, do, or have comes from love.

The positive force of love can create anything good, increase the good things, and change anything negative in your life.

Every day, in every moment, you make the choice whether to love and harness the positive force—or not.

The law of attraction is the law of love, and it is the law that is operating in your life.

Whatever you give out in life is what you receive back in life.

Give positivity, you receive back positivity; give negativity, you receive back negativity.

Life doesn't happen to you; you receive everything in your life based on what you've given.

Whether your thoughts and feelings are good or bad, they return as automatically and precisely as an echo.

People who have great lives think and talk about what they love more than what they don't love!

Talk about the good news of the day. Talk about what you love.

And bring what you love to you.

You have an unlimited ability to think and talk about what you love, and so you have an unlimited ability to bring everything good in life to you!

Love, because when you love you are using the greatest power in the universe.
~Rhonda Byrne (*The Power*)

Date Not Recorded

Here's a few quotes from a collection that I printed out and tucked in the back of my journal:

Our greatest glory is not in never falling, but in rising every time we fall.
~Confucius

It's not whether you get knocked down; it's whether you get back up.

~Vince Lombardi

That which does not kill me makes me stronger.
~Friedrich Nietzsche

When one door closes, another door opens; but we so often
look so long and so regretfully upon the closed door, that we
do not see the ones which open for us.
~Alexander Graham Bell

Each of us has a spark of life inside us, and our highest
endeavor ought to be to set off that
spark in one another.
~Kenny Ausubel

Don't give up when you still have something to give.
Nothing is really over until the moment you stop trying.
Author Unknown

Date Not Recorded

A friend shared this beautiful poem shortly after Aaron's passing. I printed it and tucked it into the back of my journal way
back in the early days:

Death is nothing at all

I have only slipped away into the next room

I am I, and You are You

Whatever we were to each other, that we still are.

Call me by my old familiar name

Speak to me in the easy way you always used.

Put no difference into our years.

Wear no forced air of solemnity or sorrow.

Laugh as we always laughed at little jokes we enjoyed
together.

Play, smile, think of me, pray for me.
Let my name be ever the household word it always was.

Let it be spoken without effect, without the ghost of a shadow
on it.

Life means all that it ever meant.

It is the same as it ever was.

There is absolutely unbroken continuity.

Why should I be out of mind because I am out of sight.

I am but waiting for you for an interval somewhere very near.

Just around the corner, all is well.

~Henry Scott Holland

Date Not Recorded

I believe my cousin shared the following with me, and I love
the sentiment behind the idea of saying yes. Because there's a
few things in life that no matter how much we want to, we
cannot change. And then our choice becomes resistance (and
all the negativity that flows from holding that attitude) or yes
(and all the blessings, knowledge, and surprises that flow from
an attitude of acceptance).

This summer I taught a Shero's Journey retreat at Hollyhock, the magical retreat center on Cortes Island in British Columbia—an island wild enough to be home to wolves and cougars. My sweetheart, Bob, came along while I taught a powerhouse group of shimmering Shero's. He birded and kayaked—until the third morning of the retreat, when he pulled a muscle in his back while kayaking.

Our friend, neuropsychologist, Buddhist teacher, and author, Rick Hanson, was also teaching at Hollyhock. Being with Rick reconnected Bob and me with life-changing practices from Rick's books, *Buddha's Brain* and *Just One Thing*. We had shared these beloved practices when we were first falling in love, a time when Bob tasted meditation and yoga for the first time.

One powerful practice Rick teaches is saying yes. This means simply saying yes to whatever is happening in this moment, whatever thought you are having, whatever emotion is passing through your awareness. Not just the peace and love and harmony, but the icky, gritty, nasty stuff as well.

As Rick writes in *Just One Thing*, "Your yes means that you accept the facts as they are, that you are not resisting them emotionally, even if you are trying with all your might to change them."

Based on this practice, Bob decided to say yes to the pulled muscle in his back. He decided to say yes to his pain, yes to the fear he'd be laid up for months, yes to his kayak resting on the pebbled beach, yes to missing yoga, yes to missing birding, hiking, and even sex (sigh).

Guess what? His back healed in a quarter of the time it usually takes.

Yes, he was relaxed, able to stretch, meditate, and be nourished by Hollyhock's amazing food and loving vibe. Yet even in paradise, he could have so easily chosen to tighten up with resentment at "missing out" on his planned retreat. Instead, he said yes. It was inspiring to behold. And it shifted everything for him.

So I ask you, where does resistance show up in your life? What might change for you today, what might open, soften, and shift, if you said yes? Yes to being late. Yes to your breakfast. Yes to a difficult client. Yes to a fabulous client. Yes to learning your mother has dementia. Yes to a stranger holding your hand and telling you it's going to be ok. Yes to being tired. Yes to a stain on your favorite shirt. Yes to the sparkle in your beloved's eye. Yes to dirty dishes. Yes to the sun spilling across the floor. Yes to the dust bunnies the sunlight illuminates.

Yes.

Saying yes is not about resignation. Resignation is a big NO, a tightening of your soul into "Everybody else can have _____ except me." Yes is the opposite. It is an opening. You simply stop opposing what you are experiencing. You notice what is. Yes creates relaxation and energy to move forward into action, out of resignation, judgment, and mind-numbing fear.

Say yes grudging, say yes fervently, say yes tentatively—there are many flavors to agreeing to have this experience you are having right now. Please do not force anything. When you do not want to say yes, when you hate the very idea, when all you want to do is scream, "NO," say yes to that too!

I'll be saying it right along with you.

~Jennifer Louden (Reprinted with permission.)

Journal Two

1/18/2020 - Shirley

I received a phone call from my daughter-in-law, Mallory, sobbing over the sudden passing of her grandma, Shirley. On Monday, Shirley was fine, and by Wednesday night, she died with Mallory and her family holding her hands.

Mallory dearly loved her grandma, and Shirley and I formed an early truce over Mallory's love of both of our cooking skills. I last saw Shirley shortly before Christmas, and we shared a brief conversation and exchanged some smiles. And now she was gone.

I told Mallory that I'd try to make her some of the things she liked that came out of the cookbook Shirley wrote out for Mallory at her request a couple years before she married my stepson, Matthew. It really didn't seem like enough of course.

On Friday of the week of her passing, Dan and I went to the visitation. That night, exhausted from a week of travel, I later fell asleep on the couch. Around 1 a.m., I had a dream that I was hugging one of Mallory's sisters at the visitation. I immediately began to awaken, and before I opened my eyes, Shirley's smiling face appeared. I said to her,

"I'm sorry about what happened." And she replied with a broad smile on her face, "It's OK. I'm fine now." In between those two brief sentences, there was a short chuckle—kind of a low "eh-eh-eh." I don't know whether that chuckle was characteristic of her or not—and I may never know, but it sure was nice to experience that visitation and feel assured that Shirley was alive, well, and happy.

When I shared my dream visitation with Mallory, I asked her if Shirley chuckled in that way. She immediately said, oh yes, that was her way of laughing. I was glad for that validation for both Mallory and me.

Date Not Recorded - Nancy

I didn't know Nancy in life, but I came to know her when I processed her obituary to our Facebook page and when I copied her memorial folders for her graveside service. A pretty lady, Nancy was deeply loved and admired by her family, business associates, and her church friends. When a butterfly lingered over the tent at her graveside service, I knew I had to let her daughter know after the service was over. You see, her daughter had worn a shirt with butterflies on it, and even had on a pair of dainty, dangling earrings in the shape of butterflies. I felt sure her mom was letting us all know she was alive and well on the other side and that her daughter's symbol for her mom would be the butterfly. But what I really didn't want to tell her was that the butterfly that showed up over the tent while the attendees were sharing their memories of Nancy was black. I worried she might not like the idea of that color being symbolic of her mom, but I'm no good at prevaricating, so after the service when I saw the daughter was alone, I went up to her and asked, "Did your mom like butterflies?" She immediately responded, "Oh yes, and so do I!" "Well, one hovered for quite a while over the tent while you were all sharing your memories of her" I said. "He was a big, beautiful black one with iridescent blue flecks. I think that might be your sign. Watch for butterflies. She'll be giving you signs using them."

The gratitude brimmed over in her eyes and she thanked me profusely. I still worried that I maybe shouldn't have told her about the butterfly's color, but about 10 minutes later, she came marching back up to me, holding up her phone, and sharing her screen saver with me… a very large black butterfly with iridescent blue flecks. It was my turn to tear up. I'm so thankful I didn't hold back the information for it was a blessing to both her and me.

In February of 2020, just before COVID 19 struck the U.S. in full force, I left my 40+ year career in financial services and joined my husband, Dan, in working at our funeral home and cemetery. We had just finished building the new funeral home in the middle of our beautiful 30-acre cemetery, and it was breathtaking to learn a new business—especially one that enabled us to touch people's lives so deeply at such a tender time. The memory of Nancy's graveside service and the beautiful black butterfly made a lasting impression. It was my first time standing on duty at a service. It was such an honor in so many ways.

5/31/2020 - Ten Years

I wrote the following tribute for Aaron on the 10th anniversary of his accident:

A single white feather floats down from nowhere out of the sky and gently lands on a knee. A bluebird pecks at the bay window a dozen times a day for two straight weeks. A giant dragonfly hovers directly overhead, and above that, a rainbow lounges in a bright blue sky. A horse sheds tears as I'm reminiscing with his person. I queue up a song on my iPod, press play, and a song called "Near to You" comes on instead.

On this, the 10th anniversary of the day my son, Aaron's, earthly life ended, I'm reminded of the ways in which I found hope, faith, and solace in the midst of staggering grief and heart-wrenching disappointment. The small signs and gentle nudges when nature didn't act natural; the dream-visitations where I'd wake up still feeling his hug, smelling his scent, and *feeling overwhelmed with his words, "You were a really good parent, Mom;" a complete stranger saying just the right thing at just the right time —a balm to my soul. These touches helped me through my darkest days and eventually filled the pages of a journal.*

Everyone's grief journey is unique, but what I do know is that more often than not our loved ones somehow find ways to let us know they're alive and well on the other side. Be on the watch, open your heart and your mind to the possibility, and don't be afraid to ask that special person to touch you in a singular way.

I'll never stop missing him and I'll never stop loving him, but these gentle yet extraordinary touches helped me learn to carry the grief, knowing he's alive and well on the other side and that I'll see him again one day when I, too, leave my earthly home.

On the 10th anniversary of your passing out of our time I was reminded of the words of Cold Play's "Till Kingdom Come" where the artist talks about hearing their loved one laugh and sing, how he wouldn't change a thing, and how he asks his loved one to wait and to set him free one day. Look it up—it's worth reading.

Date Not Recorded - "Tal"

I came down with a stomach bug a week ago, and by 10 p.m. that night I was thrashing, writhing, and whining with severe, sharp stomach pains and regular bouts of running to the bathroom. Sometime in the middle of the night, aware that I was keeping Dan awake, I crept off to the back guest bedroom. I remember talking to my spirit guide—asking if I was going to die, in fact—and suddenly he was at the back window letting me know his name is "Tal," and no, I wasn't going to die.

I don't make this stuff up.

I really wish I had written more about that entry because

the memory is foggy to me now three years later. I suspect I had a dream visitation, or perhaps I was in some heightened state due to my agony where the veil between the worlds was thin enough for me to have a semi-awakened experience. At any rate, I remember telling Dan about "Tal" the next morning, and feeling glad that I finally knew my head spirit guide's name. And of course, I survived the stomach bug to talk about it!

6/8/2020

Darkness can be so complete, and fear always hungry for a
reason.
~Author Unknown

Magical, beautiful moments that mysteriously fall from the
universe as we go along.
~Author Unknown

7/15/2020

I met the family today at the matriarch's funeral which was held graveside. Three generations of her girls were there: daughter, granddaughter, and great granddaughter. I shared briefly with them my loss of Aaron and told them that he let me know he was alive and well on the other side many times.

As we were talking, a very large bumblebee flew up behind the daughter and was smelling the flowers. I pointed this out, and all three girls nearly screamed as in unison they said, "Bee was her nickname and she loved bumblebees!" They then pointed to her grave marker and showed me where her nickname, Bee-Bee, was engraved.

At the same service, a little nine-year-old girl was watching a little butterfly as it flitted around the crowd. She extended her hand and it came to light on one of her fingers. It would flit off, but then come right back.

*She was thrilled. While the adults were engrossed in their own
conversation, I overheard the little girl softly say to herself,
"They never do this in our yard."*

I love the innocence of that remark, "They never do this in our yard." It's my belief that when we're experiencing sincere and heartfelt grief, that we somehow "vibrate" at a stronger level and are much more apt to be able to connect with those across the veil. And I believe those who've crossed over are able to manipulate things in our world in order to give us a gentle nudge to let us know they're right there seeing us and caring for us.

Date Not Recorded - Shirley

My daughter-in-law, Mallory, whom I spoke of earlier when her grandma, Shirley, passed away was having a pretty tough first pregnancy. I felt bad for her and wanted to provide comfort somehow. Remembering that I'd told her I'd make her some of her grandma's recipes from time to time, I decided to make a Chicken Log Roll from Shirley's recipe collection that I thought Mallory would enjoy. My rather voluminous recipe collection looked like a twister had passed through and I was having a really hard time putting my hands on the log roll recipe. I stopped and closed my eyes and silently asked Shirley to help me find it. It only took a second to make the request, and I opened my eyes determined to find the recipe, come hell or high water. Well, I didn't have to wait at all because it seemed as though my hand was guided and I instantly plucked that very recipe out of the mess! I smiled and thanked Shirley, and as I reviewed the recipe, I noticed at the bottom she had written to Mallory, "I know you love this because you always ask me to make it."

The next day I was sitting at a restaurant with Dan when out of the blue, Elvis' "I Can't Help Falling in Love with You" came on. That was one of Shirley's favorite songs, and was one that Mallory and Matthew had thoughtfully played at their wedding in her honor. But that wasn't all —later that day while driving alone in the car, the song came on again! A song from the 1950s heard two times in one day seems beyond coincidence in my book! And just a couple of days later as I was hunting for something in my office, I slipped my hand in a folder and behold the only thing in it was Shirley's memorial card with her photo looking right back at me!

I really felt like Shirley was all around me and had found a conduit to Mallory through me. I'm happy to be of service and, hopefully, of some comfort.

3/15/2023 - Janene

On Sunday, March 8, Janene, a good friend, unexpectedly collapsed on the front lawn while mowing grass at her sweet little cabin in the Appalachians. She was found a day later by passers-by with her faithful dog, Bella, still standing guard nearby. Another dear friend, Cathy, sped over when she heard the news. A long-time yoga practitioner and teacher, Cathy immediately observed that somehow Janene had managed to flip herself onto her back and was lying in repose in the yogic "corpse pose," arms outstretched at her side with her palms up. Janene was a deeply spiritual person, and it's quite notable that she appeared to have not only possessed an understanding of what was happening to her, but had the strength, determination, and acceptance of her fate to place herself in that sacred pose at the end of her time on earth.

It didn't end there, though. Cathy scooped up Bella and brought her home where she lovingly administered overdue insulin for the aging dog's diabetic condition.

Cathy worked for days to find a loving home for Bella, and to raise money for her ongoing care and support. During that time, Janene appeared to Cathy in her dreams, assuring her she didn't expect her to keep Bella, but appreciated what she was doing to help secure a good home for her.

Grieving for her friend, Cathy was reminded of a chapter in Autobiography of a Yogi that focused on death. She and Janene had enjoyed that book very much, and Cathy had Janene's copy of the book in her yoga studio. After her morning meditation where she chanted and lit a candle for Janene, she picked up the book and began thumbing through it for a specific passage on death she had read before. As it is a very long book, Cathy consulted the table of contents, but couldn't locate anything to guide her to the part she was seeking. She began thumbing through the pages when the book flopped open to page 416, where a beautiful cutout that perhaps Janene, who was a fabulous artist, had made. And on that page was the very content Cathy had been searching for. Divine peace settled over her. Too coincidental to be chance—Cathy knew her friend was still there!

I always recommend that people watch for those little signs from their loved ones who have passed on. I've observed that when we are in a heightened emotional state, such as grieving, we are better able to pick up on the signs and wonders from beyond this world. Rather than discounting them as mere coincidences, we can offer up a word of gratitude or prayer of thanks that our loved one cared enough about us to move heaven and earth to let us know his or her spirit is alive and well. Then, just keep watching for more.

3/18/2023 - Judy

Dan and I traveled to horse camp this weekend. We had brought all four horses which necessitated us bringing two horse trailers since our big living quarters trailer holds only three. About 17 miles outside camp, my trailer experienced a blowout. Oddly, I'd had a premonition this was going to happen. I was able to pull over safely into an empty lot. Amazingly, an unmarked police vehicle—a large truck driven by a plain-clothes policeman—pulled in behind me, blue lights flashing. He had seen the blowout and wanted to make sure I made it to safety. When Dan pulled up in the big trailer, they both remarked that they saw my trailer wheels lock up, which meant it was more than just a common flat. Perhaps bearings, brakes, brake controller, or other time-consuming, expensive stuff. Just then I glanced up, and amazingly, right across the road was a repair shop. Dan walked over, and the owner agreed to take a look and make any needed repairs. What are the chances of that?

We ferried the horses to camp in the living quarters trailer two by two and took the small trailer across the street, unhitched it from my vehicle, and headed to camp—three-plus hours later than anticipated, but everyone was safe.

While setting up camp, Dan met a neighboring camper and quickly introduced me to her, saying, "I've met someone I think you'll really like." I actually like almost everyone we meet, but Dan was right; Judy was indeed a rare gem. Judy was an avid learner, exceptionally spiritually aware, a deep thinker, and a budding animal communicator. We instantly struck up a friendship. Due to the fact that Dan had to continually travel back to the shop to check on the progress of the trailer repair, Judy and I got to spend quite a lot of time together over the weekend talking and sharing stories and ideas. Judy generously communicated with my mare, Ruby, and a number of actual facts emerged which was exciting. One day, we invited Judy to take a short ride with us and we enjoyed our time out on the trails together.

On Saturday as Dan and I were sipping our drinks by the campfire just before turning in for the night, Judy stopped by. Our conversation somehow ventured into a more personal realm and Judy began relating the story of how she'd lost her adult son three years ago to a motorcycle accident. I glanced up at Dan at that point and said, "I haven't told her." He nodded and excused himself, giving Judy and me time to talk mother to mother.

As I listened to her story, I knew I had to reveal that I too had lost an adult son to a vehicular accident.

I've told my story dozens of times over the nearly 13 years since Aaron's accident, and I'm very conscious of sharing in a soft and caring way. But I almost never break down. Yet that night, firelight flickering at our knees, Judy and I shared soul to soul. I cried and sobbed, and at times I couldn't even get the words of the story out. All the while, Judy held my hands fast in hers and waited patiently for me to continue. My account of the story was quite unremarkable—I'm sure it was even difficult to understand through all the stops and starts, however, I felt 20 pounds lighter and 30 years younger when we parted ways just before midnight to retire to our respective beds. Shedding a burden I didn't know I was carrying was the most cathartic and cleansing thing that could have happened. I slept well that night and felt so joyous in the morning—as if a rain had washed me clean.

You never know when someone's going to turn up in your life with a kind word, a stunning thought, or a listening ear. I strive to be that person for others, but it's pure magic when that gift is bestowed upon me. I am filled with awe at the synchronicity and perfect timing of meeting this sweet human who carries a burden so like my own, and who in her quiet grace was able to lift some of mine.

3/20/2023 - Your Birthday

Today would have been your 33rd birthday. How I would love to see you as a young man in your 30s. I had no expectations for what today would or wouldn't hold, but you seemed to have had quite a different idea.

I walked into the kitchen this morning and glanced out one of the windows overlooking the pasture when I noticed a small, dark streak on the screen. Upon investigation, imagine my surprise after more than a week of below-freezing temperatures every night to find a small dragonfly clinging to the screen! How could it be when we haven't seen a butterfly, dragonfly, or hummingbird yet this season in these cold temps? I smiled and offered a silent thanks to my son for sending me a little nudge with this special symbol on this special day.

As I moved around the house all day, I kept glancing over at the little dragonfly to make sure he was still there and I smiled inwardly every time I thought about the possibility that Aaron had orchestrated his appearance.

What I didn't expect to see awaited me in one of the guest rooms—the one I'd named "Remember" due to the memorabilia of various family members (including Aaron's) that it contained. Walking into that bedroom with an armload of towels I intended to put away, my jaw dropped upon seeing another dragonfly, this time a larger, double-winged one, clinging to that window screen! What were the chances?

I texted a dear friend with the story of the dragonflies on this special day and her immediate reply was, "I don't believe in coincidences." I liked that assurance because like nearly everyone else, I have a flickering faith and had begun to chip away at my own joy by worrying that their appearance was just chance.

When Dan came home after work, I immediately showed him the little dragonfly who still clung to the screen. The double-wing fellow had left, and I expected the little dragonfly to also be gone when I woke up the next morning after an even colder night of below freezing temps. However, there he clung, steadfast, and probably quite cold. I worried he might not be alive, but I touched his little body and he arched with what seemed like pleasure at my touch. As the day unfolded, it grew sunny and warm and one of the dogs wanted to go out, so I opened the back door for her. Approximately 30 minutes later, I went onto the back deck and found the dog lying in the sun…. with the little dragonfly perched on her collar! That's not something that happens every day, I thought to myself.

Figuring I'd never see the dragonfly again after the dog got up, later that day I noticed he'd navigated back to his spot on the window screen. He remains there today, two days after Aaron's birthday and continues to feel like a gift from my son.

Another friend to whom I told this story again reminded me of Albert Einstein's famous words: "Coincidence is God's way of remaining anonymous."

We really can trust and believe that these little sweet touches from our loved ones who've crossed over are real.

I was filled with joy and gratitude for the sweet and merciful "nudge" from Aaron on his birthday and throughout his birthday week. The dragonfly has been our symbol for Aaron since the day of his funeral when we began seeing them all over the place and continue to do so to this very day.

And I suppose it's also no coincidence that the day after Aaron's birthday is the Spring Equinox—a very spiritual and sacred time in our four seasons.

4/6/2023 - Jorge and Lewis

It's said that our actions—and our thoughts—ripple out into the universe. They are believed to affect those around us, either for the better or the worse, and they boomerang back to us in a karmic manner, both in this life and in the next. Well, today was a day for honesty and goodwill.

I had a large grocery shop to do as we will have 17 people here for Easter on Sunday. I generally like to use the self-checkout at the store since my groceries are then bagged the way I want. The store I visited today, however, had a particularly onerous system that repeatedly got hung up during the self-checkout process causing multiple delays and necessitating a store employee to come over and untangle the problems. By the time I was finished, I was a little edgy and was anxious to get out of the store. As I was wheeling toward the door, I glanced down in my cart and noticed three items in the upper portion of the cart that were unbagged and obviously unpaid for. I certainly didn't want to have another self-checkout experience, and several options flashed through my mind: carry on and pay for them next time I visit the store, jump into one of the lines where a cashier could check me out, suffer the self-checkout process again, or the option I finally landed on—go to customer service and see if they could quickly let me pay for the items and be on my way. The woman behind the counter seemed surprised when I told her what had happened, and she thanked me for being honest. That felt sort of good, and soon I was on my way home, the incident in the rear-view mirror and all but forgotten.

When I arrived at home, our yard crew was here for the weekly mowing. I greeted Jorge, the lead man, who speaks very little English. After a brief conversation, he asked, "Can you please help me with a problem?" I said, sure, and followed him to his lawn truck where he pulled out a black wallet. In Spanglish, he conveyed to me that he had eaten lunch at a little Mexican restaurant in our town right before coming to my house. He said he saw the wallet lying on the ground, picked it up, and put it on the console in the truck. He underscored the fact that he did not look at the money inside, but only looked at the address on the owner's driver's license. "The man lives an hour away," Jorge said. "Can you help me find him so he can get his wallet back?" I knew it was pointless to ask him why he didn't simply take the wallet into the restaurant, but I agreed to help.

Back in the house in front of my computer, I was able to find the man's name and a phone number. (I really didn't want to paw through the wallet either.) I called the number and voila, the wallet owner was found! He said he'd called the restaurant, but they had told him no one had turned it in, and I explained that I wasn't sure why Jorge didn't do that, but that he had very much wanted to ensure that the wallet was returned to its rightful owner 100% intact.

Later that day, Lewis, the owner of the wallet, drove over to pick up his wallet. He shook my hand, thanked me, and handed me a $20 bill asking

*me to give it to Jorge as a reward, which was exactly what I had been
hoping he would do (and which I had intended to do myself if Lewis
didn't). Jorge was very excited to receive the $20, and said, "Thank you,
berry, berry much!"*

It felt to me that one act of honesty and kindness immediately
boomeranged another act of honesty and kindness. Jorge had
probably found the wallet around the same time I paid for the
overlooked groceries. And while this story really has very little
to do with Aaron or anyone else who has crossed over, I do
think that when we are in sync with the cosmos (of which our
loved ones who have passed are also still a part), we can help
usher in light, love, and peace. I hope and trust Lewis will pay
it forward too.

5/4/2023 - Heinz

*A dear friend of mine was contemplating a move from her home in
Florida to a new one in North Carolina. She'd lost her husband, Heinz,
just about two years prior, and a move to NC was something they'd both
dreamed about for their retirement. After quite some time searching, Wendy
found a lovely home, put an offer in, and was finally under contract. At
first, she was super excited, but then as the days and weeks wore on, she
became extremely anxious as she thought about packing, leaving the home
she and Heinz had built, saying goodbye to her friends, transporting her
animals to the new home, and essentially starting all over again learning a
new area. After waffling back and forth a few times, she put a stake in the
ground and said she was going forward with the move and had peace
about it.*

*As she and I talked about things, I wasn't so sure she really did feel settled
about the decision. I suggested a couple things to her to help her sift
through her thoughts, but I also strongly encouraged her to reach out in her
mind to Heinz and see if he might provide some direction. She told me she
thought of him and kept up a mental chatter with him all the time, but I
had suggested that while she was lying in bed and resting before sleep*

came that she should very specifically ask him to come to her in a dream visitation and offer her his wisdom. She told me that as a scientist, these types of concepts were difficult for her to accept, but I pointed out that she had nothing to lose by merely trying.

This morning I found the following email from her in my inbox:

"Remember when you and I talked about how it would be an idea to talk with Heinz about moving? Well, I didn't talk to him before I slept, but I dreamed about him. I was in tears when I saw him and he was smiling that big Heinz smile. He's OK. He said, 'Bleib, Schatz'. *

That was strange because we rarely spoke German. I was so deep into the dream that when I awoke, I felt for a moment that I was still with him. That faded, of course, though. When I walked the dogs, I found a feather which is another sign for me. Know that you helped me spiritually to believe that Heinz and other loved ones are always around. I look forward to reading your book someday. I thought about Heinz's words and those eyes of his and decided to step back from the contract. I'm still feeling energized by his dream visit!"

* "Bleib, Schatz" means "Stay, honey" in German.

There's so much more to life than what we see right in front of our noses and from what we've learned at the end of our noses reading books and whiteboards. Albert Einstein knew it, and as I've mentioned previously, we're just scratching the surface of more knowledge that narrows the gaps between time and space, now and the future, life and death, etc. that it is crazy to cling to the notion that there's not a lot more possibilities.

I'm glad Wendy had that experience, and I trust she'll continue her dialogue with Heinz who now has the benefit of the wide view!

If you're interested in learning more, some of Stephen Hawking's works are pretty accessible. *A Brief History of Time,*

The Theory of Everything, and *Brief Answers to the Big Questions* are all decent places to start. You can also do a simple Internet search on Albert Einstein's theories (there's more than just relativity), and others' theories, such as Chaos Theory, The Butterfly Effect, and the laws of thermodynamics. And Nassim Haramein's YouTube, *The Connected Universe*, and other physics discussions are absolutely riveting.

5/28/2023

I always feel such dread when Memorial Day weekend is approaching. I really don't know what to say or do or even how to be. And it stinks that Memorial Day usually lands on a calendar date other than Aaron's actual death date of May 31, so there's really two days to observe. As the weekend creeps up on us, I can feel my family and friends watching me. I know it's from a place of love and concern, but I always feel uncomfortable thinking that others are waiting, watching, and wondering if I'm going to implode. If Memorial Day weekend were a whiteboard, I'd take that felt eraser and do away with it as quickly as I could and just start over with a clean, white, fresh slate.

My dear sister-in-law, Kellie, was living in the apartment over our garage on May 31, 2010. She lived that nightmare right along with us, up close and personal. This year, she texted me and Dan on the Friday before Memorial Day just to let us know she was thinking of us. I liked that because it was a soft approach and it didn't tear my heart to ribbons, but at the same time let me know she still remembered and cared. I texted her back a thank you and a heart emoji and attempted to put it out of my mind by going back to some house chores I was engaged in. We had Pandora playing—probably John Prine Radio or something like that— when seconds after I read and responded to Kellie's text, "Simple Man" by Lynyrd Skynyrd came on. It stopped me in my tracks. I played it at Aaron's funeral. And it was a song that I had always told Aaron I wanted him to play at mine. I had first introduced Aaron to that song when he was just a little boy. I told him how much I loved the words and how much I wanted him to live by the thoughts expressed in that tune.

And that's how this Memorial Day weekend began. Thirteen years hence. Coincidence that in an ocean of songs, "Simple Man" comes on just after I received my first acknowledgement of the weekend from someone who dearly loved that song and knew exactly how much it would mean if it played instantly after our text exchange? I don't think so. And I thanked Aaron silently from my heart for that sweet nudge.

I chose the playlist for Aaron's funeral very carefully and deliberately. It consisted of the following. I hope you'll look them up and give a listen:

- "Till I Can Gain Control Again," Willie Nelson & Kimmie Rhodes
- "Simple Man," Lynyrd Skynyrd
- "Amazing Grace," Willie Nelson
- "For Dotsy," Edgar Meyer

5/31/2023

Today marks 13 years since Aaron's accident. I've been feeling washed out and worn down all weekend, but today awoke with a lighter feeling about me. Perhaps it was because I dreamed of him last night—he was a very little boy again in the dream—or perhaps it was because Dan and I had a long discussion before I fell asleep, and he helped me realize that I don't need to go down a rathole every Memorial Day weekend—particularly when I know that Aaron is well, and he connects with me quite frequently to give me those little nudges that mean so much.

I set about my morning routine after Dan left for work, and was doing my sit-ups when I spotted something under my jewelry armoire. This is strange in and of itself because anyone who knows me well knows that I'm obsessively neat and tidy. I regularly vacuum and mop under that armoire, and I can assure you there's been nothing lying under there—until today.

I stuck my hand under the legs of the armoire and pulled out a rubber bracelet. Inscribed on the bracelet was "What Would Lamar Do?" You see, Lamar was a very dear friend and a funeral director at our business until two years ago when he quite suddenly passed away. We all were devastated, and I had the bracelets made for us to pass out at his funeral. I put mine away in a little box in one of the armoire drawers and haven't had it out in at least 18 months. I just held it in my hand and stared at it, incredulous that it would turn up today.

About an hour later while I was doing some outdoor chores, I mused to myself, "I wonder what Lamar would do today anyway if he were me?" And the answer instantly flooded my heart: "Be happy." And so, I am.

Happy to have had Aaron, happy we were in a good place relationship-wise when he left our time, happy that I have a loving family surrounding and supporting me, and most of all, happy for those dreams, visitations, and little nudges from Aaron.

Faith is not the clinging to a shrine but an endless pilgrimage
of the heart.
~Abraham Joshua Heschel

Conclusion

As I said at the start, this is a true story. A tale of my grief journey that I was lucky enough and stubborn enough to write down along the way. Some incredible things happened—things that defy logic, scientific "laws," and black and white truth as we're taught it.

I came to realize that there's more to all this than living for a while and not really knowing why and then evaporating into nothingness. My learned sensibilities want to keep telling me it's all just a black and white scientific deal, but my soul and my experiences say otherwise.

My purpose for giving my story to others is to spark hope. Because this all happened, this is all real, and everything is going to be alright. After all, Aaron said it*: "It's not like we're not going to see each other again!"

*Aaron "said" that during a psychic communication that a friend of mine generously offered to make with him. The transcript from those two conversations is included in the Supplement entitled, *Christine's Readings with Aaron*. I jotted down her words furiously as she conveyed to me what she and

Aaron had discussed. Thus, you'll note the poor grammar and flip-flopping between persons. I left it as is in here because I didn't want to polish anything and then worry about losing the meaning of what she was conveying.

Supplement

Lady

I'm fortunate that of the four of Dan's and my kids, my son, Aaron, would occasionally consent to ride with me. He would always ride my mare, Lady, whom he knew would keep him just as safe as if he were in my own arms. He always enjoyed stopping to smell the roses when we were on a trail ride, often asking if we could take a spur trail down to the lake, or to ask if we could jump off and get a photograph by a tree he liked. These trips were precious to me. He was sharing my hobby and that was such a gift.

This old, grainy photo is a favorite of mine from a day when Aaron and I rode horses together at Morrow Mountain. At the end of our ride as I was driving out of the park with the horses behind us in the trailer, I felt my heart swell when Aaron told me how much he thought of me and how glad he was that we'd had a chance to spend the day together doing something we both enjoyed.

In 2021 at exactly 25 ½ years of age, Lady passed out of our time while I held her dear head in my lap. It hurt so badly that I could hardly swallow over the lump in my throat as she left our earthly realm. I once again turned to my comforter, my solace, and my grief companion—writing. I penned the following eulogy to and for her. It speaks to the bond we shared and the hope for our future.

Sundrop's Black Lady ("Lady") - April 15, 1996 – October 15, 2021

My incomparable Lady passed out of our time on Friday, October 15. She was 25 ½ years old. She's buried here on our farm under the trees at the creek line where she loved to rest in the shade, one of her back legs cocked and head held low dozing.

I've written a eulogy TO and for her—first in my head

and now on paper—over these past couple days where the heartbreak just weighs so heavy:

I was smitten from the moment I saw you. Your pretty, small head (rare indeed for a Walking Horse!) and your jet-black coat with your flowing mane and tail on your petite 14'3 frame were a masterpiece. You took my breath away. I fell in love before I ever put a boot in the stirrup.

You'd been a broodmare so didn't know too much about what I wanted to do, but together we learned how to work with one another. You were fundamentally kind, willing, and you wanted to do right—always. I don't think it took too long before I felt that I knew your every signal. And of course, long before I came to that place, you already knew all of mine.

We had some amazing adventures together. So many rides that left indelible memories. You carried me to remote places I would have never been able to travel to on my own legs. Views from the top of a sun-drenched mountain, glades deep in the woods, snow-packed forests, and cool mountain lakes and wide rushing rivers that we waded through on blistering summer days.

We galloped for what seemed like miles neck and neck alongside Dan on Jack down an old logging road at Dupont. With Dan and Brian, we zipped and zig-zagged at a fast canter at Deep Creek, flying lead changes at every curve. I felt like we were in that forest scene in *Star Wars* and it was one of those exceptional times when we were perfectly in sync and you moved to a feather's touch. We cantered in the tunnel on The Road to Nowhere with sparks flying from your hooves as we focused on what felt like a pinpoint of light way in the distance.

And who could forget all the miles we logged just peacefully strolling through the woods with the stillness of the forest cradling us in her embrace? (Do you remember taking a spin through camp at night, bareback and with a halter tied at the nosepiece with me in my pajamas laughing at how hard you'd pace when we turned the corner to head back to our friends?

Or how you'd alert me with a soft whinny in the wee hours of the night when Jack broke his fence line and was on walkabout in horse camp?)

You carried our weight and kept us safe with your good judgment on every imaginable terrain. I remember the narrow, steep trails with a hairpin washout that you'd safely step over (while my heart felt like it was going to jump out of my chest); or coming down a mud-slicked mountain where you'd ski with your back legs to keep us steady; or when you were up to your chest navigating a rocky-bottomed icy river; and of course the time we were caught in a driving rainstorm with mud gushing at us down the trail and you were the one that took the lead and got us safely up. Yes, you had outsized courage and you would do anything I asked.

My heart ached when in your later years I had to retire you when your heaves (COPD) no longer left you with the lung power to ride the trails. And my heart broke the day we were loading the others up for a ride and you leapt in the trailer unhaltered wanting to come along. But then there was that magical Christmas two years ago when I was preparing the other horses to take my two sisters-in-law for a ride around the farm and you made it very clear you wanted me to take you too. I asked for my bridle and a leg up and the brief ride on your bare back felt as if no time at all had passed. Perhaps it was my best Christmas gift ever.

Your scent was unique. A sweet dusty odor that I always said I would recognize blindfolded. I've kept a bit of your tail hair and it now hangs at my closet door so I can inhale a part of you every morning as I start my day. I hope that in that small gesture you'll always travel with me. And maybe as a consequence I'll become kinder and more courageous. More like you. I'd like that very much.

You answered my question on Friday. But why would the end of your time here be any different? You always answered my questions in your way, didn't you?

I have only one remaining request:

Meet me at the trailhead when my time comes. I'll bring a juicy peach for you in my saddle pack. And we can travel through the silver maples up to the high meadow where perhaps we'll get a glimpse of the wild ponies. And just before daybreak, we'll visit the elk and watch them blowing in the cool air at sunrise. Dan and Jack forever at our side.

Yes, Lady, please meet me at the trailhead.

The Gift of a Poem

I recall looking up after Aaron's funeral and being astonished to see a work friend and colleague, John McKenna, standing there. He'd flown in from New York for the day specifically to attend the funeral and to show his support for me and my family. It's impossible to describe how truly touched I was by that generous gesture, and it was already becoming apparent to me that the folks I least expected to lift me up the most did and the folks I expected to provide the most comfort did not. What a strange paradox.

A short time after the funeral, I got the following via email from John:

Mary:
This poem, "Beautiful One," came to me shortly before I learned of your loss.
When the Muse left it with me, I was struck by the voice—it is different than much of my other writing—I recognized that it was different instantly. I share it with you in the same spirit that the Muse shared it with me: to lift our eyes, heart, and spirit; to remember that there remains deep mystery in God's great creation of Nature, matched in depth and brilliance with everlasting beauty.
My every wish of comfort for you and your beautiful family.
Best and warmest regards Always,
John

As if one woke once again at age six, knowing in comfort
Elemental still at six,
the sky, the stars - of course your own
the ink sky - the picture book -
more brilliant and real
the stars brighter still
and only for and to your eyes
As if once you again woke at age six
in the bliss of Nirvanic propelling belief
What would you do?
Again greet the sky; again greet the stars
And say aloud, head cast up,
"Leave me not again."

To have the sky; to have the stars pause for you
and lean to you
and greet you again and whisper,
"We have never left you,
We remain, forget not."
"Do your ears still welcome whispers?" they ask.
"Yes, I hold them like the rain"
~John McKenna ("Beautiful One")

It's astonishing to me now to read John's poem gift again all these years later and think that most often when I dream of Aaron, he's a little boy again. Not the 20-year-old young man he was that I last knew on earth, but a six to nine-year-old boy, perhaps living in what he considered to be the happiest time of his short life.

Indeed, there are no coincidences, and I am struck by the ways in which friends and other family members are often recipients of messages for us during times of grief and distress.

I'm ever thankful for John's enduring friendship and his poetic gifts and willingness to share so deeply from his soul.

Christine's Readings with Aaron

Christine talked to Aaron two times and just sat with him twice and felt him. It was a joyful place to be with him. Aaron was in a deep seat of joy—no pain from his life. There were a couple things he was sad about, but they didn't unseat him from this joyful place. His body was filled with joy—big, perfect. Aaron and Christine also talked with Sam and she is going to be just fine. At one point in the conversation, a spiritual being came into the communication to talk about Aaron's soul and his purpose. It happened when she asked Aaron if he would be coming back. She said there was a feeling of being ushered into another room. The info/being was so knowledgeable and spoke of beautiful things. Her sense is that the higher being could've even been part of Aaron's soul that was speaking. There was such peace and the words were so true it made her cry. Before their first meeting there were a couple days where Aaron said, "No, not yet" and that he was too unsteady—she explained this as a feeling of being in such high spirits that he was too excited for a conversation.

From here on, this is a transcript of what Christine captured from the conversations with Aaron. These took place sometime between June 7 and June 22, 2010:

Christine said she experienced tears of joy when talking with Aaron. She says he is in a deep seat of joy, there is no pain from his life, and his body is full of perfect joy. He spoke to her with a laughing and easygoing feeling. When she asked him what happened, he said, "I can't tell you, I'm not sure; I wish I knew too. It was as much a surprise to me as anyone. It was not planned, at least not by me. It was as if one minute I was there, then this big hand picked me up and pulled me out and then plopped me down here." She went on to say that he's starting to settle into the place where he is, but he won't be there for eternity—he is moving through things.

In her first conversation with Aaron, he said: "I don't really miss anyone either which feels so weird. I should, but I can't—they're here with me all the time. They're with me, so to miss them I'd have to feel like they were away, and they're not. I'm not in the past or in the future, just in this now sandwich where everything is here with me. I understand."

"I might try to think of something in the future like a game or a barbecue (that'll throw them off, ha), and think I should miss them because the activity won't include me being there, but I just don't feel like missing because why would I want to feel that—it's so grade school, when this feeling I have in this space right now is so much—oh it's just great. Just tell Mom it's great. It's not like I'm not going to ever see her again."

"So yes, it was a surprise. I went out to check on some things." Christine went on to explain that at one point Sam entered the conversation and said these things: "I should have been there, I'm responsible for this, I should have done something, gone along. He was just out doing something and I should have gone along. He forgot something in the woods the night before and went back to get it to find it. He couldn't sleep without going to find it. Thought it was just in the car, went out to get it, but not there and then remembered a walk, dropping it, just took off to go get it. Didn't think to take me along because he was already out there and would be right back." She also said, "I know he's not here. I was with him when he passed. I know. But I should have kept him safe. We need a lot of rest right now. Exercise for the heart, going out for a run."

Note: bracketed text is from me (Mom): [This is consistent with what we learned when we found his phone—he had called his own cell phone from the house two times around 6 a.m. We think he misplaced the phone, went to the woods and then the car to look for it, decided he might've dropped it at the grocery store the night before, and took off to go there. It's possible he found it while driving and may have even been looking down at it or rummaging for it when he lost control of the car.]

In Christine's 2nd meeting with him, he said, "But I am so sad. I can feel so sad I mean. I'm so sad for my mom, my family, for Sam. Wow, what a great life I had. I'd like some more of that. I can touch your grief; I want to help you with it, but one reason you feel it is because of me, so I don't know how to help because every thought of me makes you cry and feel terrible. And I don't want to make you feel that bad, ever. Mom, it just happened. But I don't know if I could do it over again I would change anything. This, how I feel now, is so great. I didn't know it could feel like this or everyone would want to be here. I didn't want to leave, earth is beautiful, but it's like nothing compared to whatever this is. It just fills me up. She should do whatever makes her happiness grow. [Not just me, but all of us.] Because that's what you remember here. I

139

think (at least I think I think!) and you get something in a form down below." [i.e., we can watch for small signs from him.]

Christine went on to say that Aaron felt sad to be missing all the nature, the plants, the life. Knows that Sam, Mom, loved ones, family are all in good hands and taking care of each other. Wanting to touch nature and the sun through their bodies. "I feel the sun on my face through their faces."

"Would like a memorial garden - with a few benches, chairs so they know they are not sitting there alone, they have others to be with them and where Sam can go to sit and feel the sun on her coat. A place that grounds you so I can feel it through you. And makes you happy, not sad. I want the place to make you happy because I want to feel happy, not go there to be sad with you. I just want them to be happy; that's the thing that makes me sad that I caused them this and I have to find a way to make it go away."

Christine also said at this point in the conversation he began talking about a young female he was getting close to. He said "She will have a message for you, ask her to write it down so you can have it. Welcome her in; watch for the one with the brightest laugh; hold her. I want her to know I'm OK and that I did love her."

"Sam's going to be OK. She may overdo her job to prove her worth again. I'm going to be OK, too. Just know we are always connected, the entire family, and that while I have no answers, what's more important is I'm here connected with you. Really that's what this is all about. That whether today or 50 years from now, it boils down to being connected and the joy of that. We are given that. Regardless and above all else, that can happen."

At this point in the conversation, Christine had an image of an old wise man in wisdom robes. She said it was either him (Aaron) or a saint of wisdom. He's (Aaron) going to a school now—something about wisdom, and he's coming back to study in ancient places of wisdom and as a wise man to help guide the world along with others. This is his next step. When I see him again, I will know. "She will know me as a grown man."

She (Christine) said that someone else entered the conversation at this point—a larger spiritual being—and said, "This was a taste for this young man of how to live in a loving relationship and yet be independent. To love his fellow peers and yet have a sense of self. He's [going] back quickly as to not forget who he is and needs to do to accomplish his/our/earth's purpose. To learn now and then restart again so he can be in the right place at the right time and not too burdened down with the earth life responsibilities, what happens to you/us is we can forget our connection. He was plucked, but not unkindly, so the person/time/place can align as needed. This short trip was all about love, not longevity. Love filled him up, he was to be filled up with love so his next arrival knows the purity of that and soul's body is filled up with that, not worn with love's wisdom. That will come some other time. This is love's purity that he remembers, not needing much scour pad cleaning to be completely clean, no rust on the pot, so to speak. Those around him aided in this, even amongst the hurts of life, love continued strongest prevailed. They filled him up as much as humanly possible, and this is what remains alive in him as a gift for him to contain in his next current turnaround.

In closing, Christine looked at Aaron's Chakra's and says the following:

Red – He misses being here—not the people, that is connected—but the earth's nature. Misses it with love—it's good.

Orange – Filled with love—this is what he was experiencing when they talked. Everyone's love on all levels. Fill him up with love like a tank of gasoline.

Yellow – In being alone, your true friends are attracted to you naturally—he had true friends.

Green – Let the heart be complicated. Under a stone you may find a spring of fresh water.

Heart – Crying out to say I love you back. Can you hear me?

3rd Eye – Just a veil that separates us. Christine said he was showing her how close he was to all of us.

Just a veil separates the two places.

Crown – The crown is actually our connection to the physical existence of our souls rather than us connecting up to the spirit, we don't reach up to God, we as God reach down to ourselves—our physical bodies.

Root – I love you back, can you hear me? (Christine said to let him know we can hear him—he needs that reassurance.) He feels so connected to all of us.

Sam's going to be OK. She gets it. Wants Mom to keep talking to her though. She is so connected to Aaron.

Maternal love is like a soft breeze over the heart [Sam says of me].

The blessing Christine shared with Aaron when they ended the conversation: Be within peace and come back soon.

I love that Aaron mentioned how beautiful it was where he is now. So many near death stories confirm that the afterlife is a magnificent and splendid place–and that we all go there despite our conceptions of a heaven and a hell. I recently learned that on his death bed, Thomas Edison, the great inventor, roused briefly from a coma, looked up at his family surrounding his bedside and said, "It is very beautiful over there." The modern luminary, Steve Jobs, just before he passed out of our time, looked up from his bed, gazed lovingly at his sisters, children, and his life partner, then looked past them and said just six words as he gazed at something in the distance: "Oh wow. Oh wow. Oh wow." While I'm not enamored with the idea of the possibility of illness that may create a painful death, I am, in Jane Goodall's words, looking forward to "the next great adventure."

Recommended Reading/Viewing

Books:

Eat Pray Love by Elizabeth Gilbert
The Eagle and the Rose: A Remarkable True Story by Rosemary Altea
Horses and the Mystical Path by Adele von Rüst McCormick, Thomas E. McCormick, Marlena Deborah McCormick
The Secret by Rhonda Byrne
The Greatest Secret by Rhonda Byrne
Proof of Heaven by Dr. Eben Alexander
On Life After Death by Elisabeth Kubler-Ross
Kinship With All Life by J. Allen Boone
Letters To Strongheart by J. Allen Boone
You Are the Adventure by J. Allen Boone
Autobiography of a Yogi by by Paramahansa Yogananda
Many Lives, Many Masters by Brian Weiss
The Tao of Equus by Linda Kohanov
Signs by Laura Lynne Jackson

Videos:

The Connected Universe (and any other material) featuring Nassim Haramein

Movies:

What Dreams May Come with Robin Williams
Dragonfly with Kevin Costner
Hereafter with Matt Damon

Music:

I'll Love You Till the Day I Die by Willie Nelson and Lukas Nelson
Everywhere I Go by Willie Nelson
New Again by Brad Paisley and Sara Evans
Till I Can Gain Control Again by Willie Nelson and Kimmie Rhodes
Run Maggie Run by Chris Stapleton
Energy Follows Thought by Willie Nelson

Afterword

I'm grateful to so many people for helping this project cross the finish line. I knew early on I wanted to publish my journals, but I never really knew what an undertaking it would be. My husband and my rock, Dan, was always encouraging. His faith has held me steady all these years. Friends also encouraged me, many times saying just the right things when I was at my lowest and most doubtful points. I'd never choose to have what happened take place, but I do think Aaron and I took on quite a project when we agreed to the script for how our lives on this earth would play out in this epoch. He's made me a better person and caused me to thereby be of better service to others.

Matthew Cross was along on this journey the entire way. He provided support just when I needed it most, and gave valuable advice that helped make the book work better. My editor, Dr. Claire King, gave smart suggestions and was generous with encouragement which is a gift beyond compare. Molly Sargent was my wing woman—she led me to some valuable resources and provided smart advice. Jessica Brink did the initial formatting of the book. It had gotten so scattered and ugly as I wrote it that I couldn't bear to look at it. She rescued it from the mud and gave it structure and a polished look. And then there were the many people who graced me with their testimonials after reading an advance copy of the manuscript. Keith Banks, an internal client and friend, said those words that launched my journaling, "Do what you feel like doing and do what you feel like doing when you want to do it." Sometimes it's the simple things that matter so much in another's life. Thinking about how deeply we can influence another human or other living being reminds me to strive towards living in accordance with The Golden Rule.

I had a really hard time with the title of this book, but early on when I began experiencing Aaron connecting with me from outside our time, I recalled an original Star Trek episode, *The Immunity Syndrome*, where Mr. Spock takes a shuttlecraft into the dangerous and toxic "zone of darkness" and loses communication with the ship. Everyone thinks he's dead until they suddenly feel and hear a bang on the outer hull of the ship at which point Captain Kirk happily shouts, "He's alive! He's kicked it in the side to let us know." That felt to me just like what Aaron was doing, and right then and there the term "nudge," felt right.

Me and Dan in the Virginia High Country

About the Author

When asked to provide biographical info, Mary's first sentence typically is, "I'm a mom." To say that Aaron was and is important to her is an understatement. She considers him her foremost gift and trusts that in providing his and her story to readers, they too will receive a gift.

Mary grew up in a small midwestern town and enjoyed an active outdoor life during an era when life was slower and simpler. A self-described lifelong learner, Mary was encouraged and unrestricted by her parents to read anything and everything that interested her. Her love for words, language, and stories persists to this day.

After college, Mary spent 41 years in financial services where she held roles in sales, leadership, and as an executive leading Learning & Development teams for Fortune 500 firms. She has a BA in Psychology and has recently graduated with highest honors from the Funeral Director's program at Fayetteville Technical Community College. She is on schedule to complete her resident trainee program in the Fall of 2023, at which time she will become a licensed North Carolina Funeral Director.

Mary lives on a small farm in North Carolina with her husband and their four horses, three dogs, four cats, and two fish. In her spare time, Mary enjoys reading, gardening, water skiing, sketching, writing, and horseback riding.

Follow Mary on her website, MaryConnaughty-Sullivan.com, or at Mary Connaughty-Sullivan on Facebook.

I'd be remiss if I didn't acknowledge Aaron as the co-author of this work. It's not just my story—it's his as well.

In his brief life, Aaron was a friend to all he met. He treated everyone with dignity and respect—and expected the same in return. Aaron had a sharp sense of humor and loved to have fun with his friends and his family. His dog, Sam, pictured below, was his pride and joy. She was devoted to him, and she has remained devoted to me all these years since Aaron left our time.

Aaron Michael Paton
3/20/1990 – 5/31/2010